V.S.Naipaul
Social Criticism in His Non-Fictional Works

Dr. Sanjay Sharma

ADHYAYAN

ADHYAYAN PUBLISHERS & DISTRIBUTORS
New Delhi-110002

Published by
ADHYAYAN PUBLISHERS & DISTRIBUTORS
4378/4B, 105, J.M.D. House, Murari Lal Street
Ansari Road Darya Ganj, New Delhi - 110002
Ph.: 011-23263018, 011-23277156, Fax: 23280028
Email: adhyayanpublishers@yahoo.com

V.S.Naipaul
Social Criticism in His Non-Fictional Works

Edition 2012
ISBN 978-81-8435-333-4

Printed in India

Published by Harish Chandra Yadav for Adhyayan Publishers & Distributors, Delhi. Laser Typesetting at Jain Computers and Printed at Tarun Offset Printers, Delhi

Dedicated

To

The Sweet and Immortal

Memory

of My Parents

(Late) Shri Hawaldar Sharma

and

(Late) Smt. Krishna Sharma

Foreword

V.S. Naipaul has been a controversial writer all through and is seen by some as a pioneer of India bashing attitude for gaining creative height in the world. The controversies show his audacious frankness in speaking his mind or in responding to his encounter with persons and places. His responses at times may not be well reasoned and are offending to Indian sensibility particularly in his *Trilogy* but they do not seem to me guided by any anti- India campaign. They are certainly provocative. But if something provokes you to delve deep into it, it is certainly a welcome sign. This might have been the case with Sanjay Sharma's doctoral work in this relatively virgin area of research. Non-fiction has always been an under-studied zone of research whereas fiction is overworked and more often the research is hackneyed. His mentor and supervisor Dr. Vinay Shanker Shukla deserves kudos for promoting original research in the area where 'angels fear to tread'. Works on V.S.Naipaul's fiction are galore but comprehensive studies on his non-fiction are few and far between, This, at the outset, makes his work relevant to the present discourse on Naipaul. The perspective of the author in the book covers almost all thematic concerns in Naipaul's non-fiction- social, political, religious and cultural and Naipaul's approach in his social criticism is summed up in ' Disinterestedness' that probes into his objectivity and unaffected critical thought. Naipaul's response to India is born out of his disillusionment about India as he came here with a romantic notion about his ancestral land. So a critic has to keep this cultural dislocation in mid while approaching his works. The author maintains it and gives a critical response to a critic rather than an emotional response. I wish his debut critical foray all success.

Dr. C.L.Khatri
Editor, Critic and Poet
Associate Professor,
Dept. of English
T.P.S. College, Patna

Preface

V.S. Naipaul remains one of the most widely read and admired literary figures of the contemporary world. He has never been shy of discussing the pains of his own position. He is the master of the art of fiction writing and it enables him to make his travelogues perfect. He is aware of the fact that he is doing something serious for which a fitting technique is required. He has his own philosophy of life and his original world view. He is a disillusioned romanticist who finds modern writers too egoistic and modern critics too pedantic to be able to relate literature to life. He finds the present day world full of contradictions and confused conditions. Naipaul's concept of travelogue is a comprehensive one. His travelogues constitute a dispassionate criticism of society. This criticism is often painful but it is always with great social relevance. His ironic vision makes his criticism sharp. Naipaul's writings have attracted critics like Walsh, White, Paul Theroux, R.H. Lee and Karl Miller, who have presented meticulous studies of his works. Naipaul's travel writings are specimens of technical perfection but this perfection is no obstacle to their quality of yielding pleasure. These books make good reading which is delightful to the scholars as well as to the common readers.

Naipaul visits various societies to explore diverse social realities. He examines the various shades of the society–individual relationship in varying situations. The contemporary political realities catch him attention and he goes deep into them with his extraordinary political acumen. The expediency of the institution of government invites him to dissect various governments and to peep into them. Religion as palpable force compels his thinking and he looks at it from various angels. The present book focuses on Naipaul's multi-dimensional approach to the contemporary world.

Contents

1

Introduction

Sir Vidiadhar Surajprasad Naipaul is one of the greatest writers of the contemporary English speaking world. His lifetime literary achievements have been of rare merit and these achievements won for him the Nobel Prize for literature in 2001. He is a novelist, a serious traveller, a competent critic and a great philosopher. His literary output is chiefly related to the cultural chaos of the so-called Third World and complications of alienation and displacement. His reputation as a novelist has overshadowed his fame as a writer of non-fiction but the fact is that most of his serious writing is to be found in his non-fictional works.

Born in Trinidad in 1932 Naipaul belongs to a family of Indian descent as well as of established literary reputation. Seepersad Naipaul, Shiva Naipaul, Neil Bissoondath, Vahni Capildeo and Nadira Alvi make his family look like a literary club. His meritorious life has been summarized in these words:

> V.S. Naipaul was knighted in 1989. He was awarded the David Cohen British Literary Prize by the Arts Council of England in 1993 and the Nobel Prize for literature in 2001. He holds honorary doctorates from Cambridge University and

> Columbia University in New York, and honorary degrees from the universities of Cambridge, London and Oxford. (*contemporary writers.com*)

Naipaul's early literary works appeared in 1950s, but these could not show the promise of the forthcoming literary achievements. His first non-fictional work *The Middle Passage* appeared in 1962. Since then he has continued to write seriously about the world and its people. Each new work has added a feather to his cap. His incisive examination of the world and his sweet and sour experiences form the core of his work. Universality is the hallmark of his works. There are references to the *Gita* and *Kama Sutra*. Rudyard Kipling, E.M. Forster, Jane Austen, Charles Dickens and William Hazlitt are discussed to differentiate between the European and the Indian sensibility. On the Indian side, Sri Aurobindo, R.N. Tagore, J.L. Nehru and Nirad C. Choudhuri are discussed. The following words taken from the Internet are relevant here:

> Everything that has ever happened to him is pigeonholed with exactitude in his memory. Formidably well-read, he can quote books he read years ago, and all the conversations he has had. Melancholy grips him at the spectacle of 'the steady grinding down of the old world' as he puts it, and he might complain to an interviewer that he is living in a 'plebeian culture that celebrates itself'. (*nobelprize. org.)*

As a travel writer Naipaul has observed the world and its people keenly. In his non-fictional works he has given his experiences in candid terms. While in his novels he presents reality couched in fiction, in his non-fictional writings he presents it directly and unreservedly. His criticism of the world is often bitter and scathing but it is never removed from truth. *The Middle Passage* is his first non-fictional work. It is an account of a visit he made to the Caribbean in 1960 after living in England for many years. Here Naipaul explains why West Indian society is the way it is, and expianation is always a first step towards understanding and sympathy.

An Area of Darkness (1964), *India: A Wounded Civilization* (1977) and *India: A Million Mutinies Now* (1990) form his Indian trilogy which has drawn the attention of readers specially in India. An understanding of Naipaul's attitude to India is essential for the understanding of his growth as a writer. He is of Indian descent and India has remained with him throughout his career as a writer. His rage, anguish and search for roots have always reffered to India, indirectly and directly. Although his criticism of India is not always friendly and sympathetic, it draws our attention to certain Indian realities which cannot be ignored. Namrata Rathore Mahanta observes.

> Thus Naipaul's writings on India are not only the outcome of his quest for identity but are also a unique record of the making of a diasporic writer, of his development, of his anguish, rage, search, and finally of his successful mental restoration of India from a pattern of painful fragmentation to wholeness. (*Trilogy* VIII)

The Loss of El Dorado, a masterly study of New World history, was published in 1969. It is history as literature meticulously researched and masterfully written as in the manner of Thucydides. Mr. Naipaul has not only given us a lesson in history, he has shown us how it is best written.

Among the Believers: An Islamic Journey (1981), a large scale work, is the result a seven months' travel in 1979 and 1980 in Iran, Pakistan, Malaysia and Indonesia. It displays all of Naipaul's major themes, his great talent as a writer and the narrowing down of his vision. On the back cover of the volume is given the following assessment of the book:

> *Among the Believers* is V.S. Naipaul's classic account of his journey through Iran, Pakistan, Malaysia and

> Indonesia; 'the believers' are the Muslims he met on those journeys, young men and women battling to regain the original purity of their faith. (back cover blurb)

Beyond Belief (1998) is a sequel to *Among the Believers*. The book has been subtitled *Islamic Excursions Among the Converted Peoples*. Naipaul collects his experiences gathered in four non-Arab Muslim countries. He is shocked by the degeneration of Islamic culture in these countries. The Prologue to the book describes its purpose thus:

> This is a book about people. It is not a book of opinion. It is a book of stories. The stories were collected during five months of travel in 1995 in four non-Arab Muslim countries - Indonesia, Iran, Pakistan, Malaysia. So there is a context and a theme. (1)

Finding the Centre (1984) is distinguished by the author's narrative on his emergence as a writer. The book consists of two personal narratives entitled "Prologue to an Autobiography" and "The Crocodiles of Yamoussoukro". The book is, in many ways, the best key to Naipaul as a writer. The Author's Foreword contains the following words:

> The two personal narrative pieces that make up *Finding the Centre* were written one after the other and occupied the best part of two years. They are offered as a book principally for that reason; and also because, over and above their story content, both pieces are about the process of writing. (9)

The Writer and the World (2002) is a collection of Naipaul's essays related to the Indian, the African and the American occasions. Here he comes before the reader as a keen student of universal civilization. The book is notable for Naipaul's rare understanding and prophetic vision of the world. The book contains an informative Introduction by Pankaj Mishra who is also the editor of the book. *Literary Occasions* (2004) is another collection of Naipaul's essays containing eleven valuable pieces. In fact, the book is a companion piece to *The Writer and the World*. It is also edited by Pankaj Mishra with an Introduction by him. The blurb of the book describes it thus:

> A remarkable companion piece to his previous volume of highly acclaimed essays, *The Writer and the World*, and sustained by extraordinary powers of expression and thought, *Literary Occasions* is a stirring contribution to the fading art of the critic, and a revelation as well of a life in letters, in its many exemplary instances. (blurb)

A Writer's People (2007) is the outcome of Naipaul's serious travel experiences. Here Naipaul acknowledges the diversity of world views although non of them may be perfect. Mahatma Gandhi, Derek Walcott, Gustave Flaubert, Vinoba Bhave and Nirad C. Choudhuri and several others are criticized unreservedly.

Most of Naipaul's non-fictional writing comprises his experiences as a traveller. He is a born traveller like Marco Polo, and Vespucci. He enjoys writing about his travels and during the course of his writing reveals several of his views on literature and the process of writing. Except Antarctica and Australia he has travelled almost all the continents. He has studied life in different parts of the world and his study compels him to write. His knowledge of men and manners, culture and civilized or uncivilized way of life is extraordinary. The Caribbean islands, India, Iran, Pakistan, Africa, America, Argentina, the Congo, Malaysia, Indonesia and the deep south of America have been travelled by him with the keen eye of an explorer. He is perhaps the greatest historian of the contemporary world. Truth provokes him to write. He is a bold critic of the world and his criticism has often angered people, specially the Indians. He hardly cares for applause or criticism. Truth is what matters for him. In fact, he is a great discoverer of ideas. For him the world is full of ideas which have to be taken note of. Their mere existence is not sufficient and they have to be seen in flesh and blood. These ideas originate a creative tension in his mind which is released in his writings. He is a great observer of the drama of life. What M.A. Goldberg says about Kafka and Camus is equally true about Naipaul's writings:

> Far from being restricted to the limiting dimensions of one's being, the adventure is always a scene from a larger drama being enacted in a theatre whose dimensions are more vast than any encompassed by the human eye or brain. It may be, as Jung contends, a psychic residuum of countless experiences of the same kind... (*Chronology* 23)

Writing is a serious vocation for Naipaul. For him it is as pious as religion. It is only through writing that he can do justice to the world as well as to his own self. His seriousness about being a writer suggests that he shares Carlyle's idea of writers as a kind of secular clergy, as prophets and moral teachers, elevated by their vocation high above other men. His message is that writers have a duty towards themselves to chart and thus find meaning in their own lives. His father also had encouraged Naipaul in his writing aspirations.

Naipaul has received tremendous critical attention. Critics and scholars have produced a considerable body of criticism on Naipaul and his works. They have tried to explore almost every aspect of Naipaul's creative genius, but none of the critical works on Naipaul's writings can be said to be perfect. *Postcolonial Situation in the Novels of V.S. Naipaul* (2004) by Champa Rao Mohan focuses on the postcolonial cultural disintegration in the East and Naipaul's vision of the world. The book pays no attention to Naipaul's non-fictional works. *V.S. Naipaul: An Introduction* (2000) by Yashoda Bhat is a handbook which studies Naipaul's expatriate sensibility and his vision of the 'New World History'. The book is of great help to a researcher. *V.S. Naipaul: The Indian Trilogy* (2004) by Namrata Rathore Mahanta focuses on the making of the writer and the evolution of his technique as a travel writer. The book does not take into account the whole body of Naipaul's travel writing. *V.S. Naipaul: Critical Essays* (2002) edited by Mohit K. Ray is a book in three volumes. It contains valuable articles by scholars like Rama Kundu, N. Sharada Iyer, Bijay Kumar Das, David Malcolm, Rafe Dalleo, and S. Kanakraj. The fact is that none of the critical essays is a complete assessment of Naipaul as a travel writer. *The Novels of V.S. Naipaul* (1990) by Shashi Kamra focuses on Naipaul's third - world consciousness. The book is of little help in a research on Naipaul's non-fiction. *India in the works of Kipling, Forster and Naipaul: Postcolonial Revaluations* (2000) by Purabi Panwar provides insight into Naipaul's approach to India. The book is of no great help in the over all estimation of Naipaul's travel writing. *V.S. Naipaul: A Literary Response to the Nobel Laureate* (2003) is edited by Suman Bala. It is a collection of recent critical essays on the works of V.S. Naipaul. *Recent Indian Fiction* (1994) by R.S. Pathak, *V.S. Naipaul* (2002) by Manjit Inder Singh, *V.S. Naipaul: Fiction and Travel Writing* (2002) edited by Rajeshwar Mittapalli and Michael Hensen and *Twentieth Century Indian English Fiction* (2004) by M.K. Naik provide scattered pieces of information about Naipaul. K.R.S. Iyenger's *Indian Writing in English* (2003), M.K. Naik's *A History of Indian English Literature* (1994) and *Dimensions of Indian English Literature* (1985). Ian Ousby's *The Cambridge Guide to Literature in English* (1992) and William Walsh's *Commonwealth Literature* (1973) are some other books of common use to researchers. Valuable critical articles are being published in different noted national and international literary journals from time to time. Ample material is also available on various websites.

A fresh appraisal of Naipaul's non-fiction is the need of the hour. The present study focuses on the objective social criticism found in Naipaul's non-fictional works, his concern for a healthy relationship between individual and society, his exploration of the role of religion in the present-day world and his analysis of the role of governments in the contemporary context.

Naipaul's approach to life has widened since the beginning of his career and it has taken into account the whole world. In his criticism of the contemporary societies he has adopted a scientific, an objective and often a ruthless stand. After Trinidad, India is the first country which catches his attention the most. The Permanent Secretary of the Swedish Academy aptly remarked:

> Naipaul's literary domain has extended far beyond the West Indian island of Trinidad, his first subject, and now encompasses India, Africa, America, from south to north, the Islamic countries of Asia and, not least England. (Ray, *Essays* Vol.III, 11)

Naipaul has studied various societies and has come to the conclusion that they have varied relations with the individual. So far as his own case is concerned he is all praise for the West as it provides the greatest possibilities to the individuals effort. In fact, it is the West which made him a writer. John Thieme remarks:

In short, personal endeavour is possible in the West and not elsewhere - or at least this is so as far as Naipaul is concerned. The Academy seems to have chosen him at this moment in time, because of his ostensible concern with the individual rather than the macro - political... (*Nobel* 6-7)

In the contemporary world almost every religion has undergone a horrible degeneration. Several of them have dwindled into religiosity and selfish creeds. Naipaul's severe criticism of Islam, in particular, has drawn the attention of the world. In his writings he has tried to underline the fact that almost all religions in their present form deserve criticism. The very concept of religion has to be viewed afresh.

The role of governments and various political systems

is equally important. It has affected the freedom of the individual and the destiny of nations. Naipaul keenly explores the role played by various governments in shaping the fate of their peoples.

Naipaul is a writer who deserves constant critical attention. He is a free critic of the world whose word matters. Whether he prefers to be called ironist or satirist, whether he really has no hope of improving society by pointing out its shortcomings, the impact of his works is the same as that made by those of Dryden, Pope and Swift. There is always at the back of his writings a sense of loss arising out of unrealized values. He is an open minded critic of the world and a free traveller. He is constantly compelled by his curiosity. Harald Leusmann pays tribute to Naipaul as a traveller in these words:

> He follows his instincts and the curiosity of a writer, not so much that of an ethnographer. Naipaul seems to be free in his movements, independent in the way he approaches persons and events and guided only by his own sympathies free of constraints. (*Trials* 73)

2

Disinterestedness

Naipaul is not only a serious traveller but also an equally serious critic of the world. As a critic he exploits his travel experiences in the best possible manner. His criticism of the world is always objective and disinterested. As he is a severe critic, his criticism may offened the readers at times, but the fact is that its objectivity and disinterestedness are never in question. His travel experiences are always at the core of his writing including his fiction. His whole body of literary writing is a rare document of social criticism. His novels cannot be separated from his travel writing. While in his novels his criticism of the world is in the form of fiction, his travel writings often read like novels. One thing is clear about his identity that he is a traveller and a critic. He constantly gathers experiences and interprets them for the benefit of readers. His writings are the products of his impressions of the world. About the link between his novels and travel writings. Serafin Roldan Santiago maintains:

> It is not certain, like the proverbial chicken and the egg, which would come first: whether the fictional elements in his travel narratives, or the travel paradigms in his fiction. Both are inextricably woven and meshed together. (*Vulcanisation* 172)

Naipaul's objectivity arises from the fact that he is nowhere at home. In fact, he is a homeless wanderer leading a nomadic life of bitter and sweet experiences. His objectivity makes him bold and unsparing. He is fond of dealing with controversies and unpleasant themes which other writers generally avoid. He not only raises issues but also solves several of the problems infesting the contemporary world. His greatness lies in the fact that he is a detached observer of the world. N. Sharada Iyer describes Naipaul as a nomadic intellectual in the article entitled "Naipaul's India - *An Area of Darkness*":

> ... Naipaul's writings dealt with the cultural confusion of the Third World and the problem of an outsider, a feature of his own experience as an Indian in the West Indies, a West Indian in England and a nomadic intellectual in a postcolonial world. (85)

Besides the contemporary cultural confusion, man's inner inconsistencies put Naipaul to bitter disillusionment. He is shocked by the chaos and skepticism of his times. Matthew Arnold felt a similar shock in the Victorian age. He is in need of a firm ground to stand on. As he can't avoid the shock he faces it boldly and comes out victorious. Santosh Chakrabarti compares his position as a writer with that of Matthew Arnold:

> What Matthew Arnold felt in the Victorian age has become more acute in the modern age with man's inner inconsistencies and existential incompatibilities exacerbating the schism. (*Alienation* 45)

As *The Middle Passage* is his first book of non-fiction, it is full of its own merits and demerits. Naipaul had already completed the first phase of his writing and he was about to begin a new form of writing which created doubts within him. He visited Trinidad and Tobago after a gap of six years on a government scholarship offered to him by the then Prime Minister Dr. William Ericks. Naipaul visited his motherland both as an insider and an outsider. *The Middle Passage* is unique in the sense as it is written by a person who has seen Trinidad and Tobago from within and without. In observing his motherland he followed his British predecessors like Trollope, Froude and Kingsley. Thus, he is more of an outsider than an insider. Yashoda Bhat holds a similar opinion:

> As an individual, Naipaul was a Victorian British, when he started writing *The Middle Passage*. There were several accounts of the Caribbean islands by writers like Trollope Froude and Kingsley. They seem to have become Naipaul's ideological masters so far as travel writing is concerned. (*Introduction* 111)

In the gap of six years several changes had taken place in Trinidad and Tobago. There was also a great change in Naipaul's attitude to his homeland. Naipaul revisited his home country with an altogether fresh perspective. Travelling is regarded as a ritual which has to be performed with all seriousness. The ship in which he travels carries a variety of ethnic groups and Naipaul's description of them reads like a novel. These groups represent the world of immigrants, symbolic of constant flux of expatriate experiences. Naipaul observes the changes and finds that inspite of these changes there is no essential difference noticable in these countries. The order established by the colonial rulers still persists. There is no political unity and no economic strength. These countries still have the look of a slave nation. The people of these islands are 'mimic men'. They imitate the imperialists although they have gained freedom. The political freedom in these countries is not complete as there is no spirit of true nationalism and cultural unity developed in these countries. Naipaul is utterly disillusioned. Several critics blame Naipaul for being a colonial observer but the fact is that he is a dispassionate critic even of his own homeland.

The Middle Passage is remarkable for its autobiographical character also. He does not feel at home in Trinidad. He feels compelled to leave as he had felt six years ago. Naipaul redefines his position vis-à-vis the Caribbean islands. He does not get reconciled to his home country and his homelessness is confirmed. His criticism of his homeland has been the subject of severe attacks from different critics but the reality is that it is never without a palpable grain of truth in it. Yashoda Bhat goes on to say:

> *The Middle Passage* confirmed his position as a travel writer but it also drew forth a lot of tirade from the natives of the Caribbean islands. Several scholars, however, saw truth in his observation. (113)

Naipaul is critical not only of his own homeland but also that of his ancestors. His criticism of India is contained in his Indian trilogy. When he visited India, he came with several dreams in his mind but what he found in reality was entirely different. He shares a similar approach to India with E.M. Forster. Forster visited India compelled by emotions. He appreciated many Indian things and criticized several others. Forster found Italy cleaner than India. As a critic Naipaul is more severe than Forster. Forster does not criticize the Indian poverty and squalor. The difference between the two is that while Naipaul has roots in India, Forster is completely a foreigner. Purabi Panwar rightly calls him a liberal humanist who constantly tries to shake off the 'white man's burden':

> He made a conscious effort to shake off the white man's burden but it stuck to him at times. Consequently, his perspective was generally that of a liberal humanist, tinged with what can be described as a restructured colonialism. (*India* 88)

Naipaul's first experience of India came as a shock to him. He found Indians rough and rude. They lacked manners and had no wish to learn them from the Britishers. They were indifferent to civil manners and they hardly cared for cleanliness. They ridiculed those who imitated the British manners. The following words clearly indicate to the slipshod way of Indian life:

> It is easy for Indians to make fun of Bunty... for his foreign interest in interior decoration; for the spotless bathroom and adequate towels he provides for his guests (such attentions in India being beneath the notice of all but the latrine - cleaner: the Indian lavatory and the Indian kitchen are the visitor's nightmare). (*Darkness* 58)

Naipaul found that India was not a land of dreams, rather this was an area full of glaring realities. His state is reminiscent of Saladin Chamcha of *The Satanic Verses* who thinks the coloured people to be the lowest of the low. Their dark colour is symbolic of their inner darkness. Naipaul's experiences of India are nightmarish but indispensable. What Joel Kuortti says about *The Satanic Verses* is true about several of Naipaul's writings:

> Saladin Chamcha, one of the novel's double protagonists, has a nightmare in which he feels sorry for the people of colour: 'Every morning you have to look at yourself in the mirror and see, staring back, the darkness, the stain, the proof that you're the lowest of the low'. (*Identification* 57)

He desired to visit the village of his ancestors in the eastern Uttar Pradesh. He had already developed a sense of separateness from India. He found the brown land near the village unfruitful. There were dull scenes all around. When he reached the village, he was fascinated by nothing. He could get no accurate information about his forefathers:

> It remained the land of my childhood, an area of darkness; like the Himalayan passes, it was closing up again, as fast as I withdrew from it into a land of Myth; it seemed to exist in just the timelessness

> which I had imagined as a child, into which, for all that I walked on Indian earth, I knew I could not penetrate. (*Darkness* 274)

India was like a hut surrounded by darkness at evening. None of his mental images could be realized and he was faced with only confusion and chaos. It was a land of darkness left behind by his grandfather long ago. The darkness still remained and nothing had changed. His grandfather's journey was one from darkness to light. Naipaul is happy that he is far away from this darkness:

> ... something of darkness remains, in those attitudes, those ways of thinking and seeing, which are no longer mine. My grandfather had made a difficult and courageous journey. It must have brought him into collision with startling sights... (24)

Naipaul is shocked by the economic, social and political condition of India. The Indian concept of spirituality does not convince him. He ridicules the Hindu concept of the world as an illusion and says that this visit to India has created a sense in him that the whole world is an illusion. In the chapter entitled "Pilgrimage" he describes his experiences at the Cave of Amarnath in these words:

> And in the cave, the god: the massive ice phallus. Hindu speculation soared so high; its ritual remained so elemental. Between the conceptions of the world as illusion and the veneration of the phallus there was no link; they derived from different strata of responses. (166)

Scholars have mentioned that Naipaul suffers from an inner contradiction. He tries his best to be objective and detached but he finds it difficult to get rid of the European values he had adopted in all seriousness. He is an Indian with a difference. He underlines the value of individual endeavour in life. His greatness lies in his objective approach to the world at large. John Thieme pinpoints:

> ... on the one hand, Naipaul is a neutral witness, uninfluenced by cultural trends, who allows events to speak for themselves; on the other, he is a writer who has found himself through his devotion to European civilization. (*Nobel* 8)

Naipaul is a diasporic writer with a difference. He is twice removed from India. India may be an area of darkness but it is indispensable for him. In fact, his past is indispensable for him. India is a great storehouse of experiences and literary material for Naipaul. What Namrata Rathore Mahanta says about the diasporic writers in general is fully true about Naipaul:

> Their roots shoot down only to strike against a frozen, fractured consciousness and then begin a search for crevasses – to anchor on to, and the diasporic literature is born. (*Trilogy* VII)

Critics hold the opinion that Naipaul's approach to India became maturer by steps. In his second visit he found the Indian civilization a wounded one. Although he is not full of perfect sympathy for India, he still considers it as a nation which has suffered great losses at the hands of its foreign rulers. He is critical of the fact that independence in India is no more than going away of its foreign rulers. Independence means something more which is missing in India. In the Forword he writes:

> India in the late twentieth century still seems so much itself, so rooted in its own civilization, it takes time to understand that its independence has meant more than the going away of the British; that the India to which Independence came was a land of far older defeat; that the purely Indian past died a long time ago. (*Wounded* X)

Naipaul holds the view that the prolonged foreign

rule in India paralysed the Indian civilization beyond all remedy. Besides ignorance, poverty and cruelty make matters worse. India has lost its old glory and lost its way into the wilderness of barbarianism. There is a chapter in the book entitled "Paradise Lost". Here Naipaul says that India is full of discrepancies which make it look like a zoo. The melancholy middle class lady in the chapter goes to the extent of saying that the Indians should charge for the entertainment they provide. The following words deserve mention:

> 'We are like a zoo,' the melancholy middle-class lady said in Delhi. Perhaps we should charge. ... India was like a zoo because India was poor and cruel and had lost its way. (122)

The foreign invasion left India wounded and removed from all its glory. The Indian self respect was replaced by obedience to others. The only major concern was to servive at any cost. With this there came an end to all free thinking and India was left without an ideology. Even after independence this lack of ideology is felt in India. Naipaul writes:

> India is without an ideology - and that was the failure of Gandhi and India together. Its people have no idea of the state, and none of the attitudes that go with such an idea: no historical notion of the past, no identity beyond the tenuous ecumenism of Hindu beliefs, ... (155)

What shocked Naipaul was the contrast between India's past glory and its present misery. India might have been a glorious nation in the past but now it was lost in the darkness of ignorance. There was no attempt on her part to regain the old glory. The Indians followed the Western ways blindly and there was hardly any hope of a bright future. Kunjo Singh observes in the article entitled "Reporting from the Journeys: V.S. Naipaul's *An Area of Darkness, India: A Wounded Civilisation* and *Among the Believers*:"

> In his visit to India Naipaul has looked hard at the reality of India. What he saw pained him, shocked him, disillusioned and enraged him. He was maddened by the smug talk of India's ancient culture and spirituality in the face of India's horrendous poverty... (98)

Naipaul never praises any Indian thing or person blindly. He never shirks from the unpleasant truths about them. He criticizes great politicians like Gandhi and Nehru, great writers like R.K. Narayan and Vijay Tendulkar and the political events like the Emergency. The kingdom of Vijayanagar in South India is praised as a great Hindu kingdom which did not surrender to the Muslim rulers. In the following words Naipaul describes the whole truth about how it was established:

> The kingdom was founded in 1336 by a local Hindu prince who, after defeat by the Moslems, had been taken to Delhi, converted to Islam, and then sent back to the south as a representative of the Moslem power. There in the south, far from Delhi, the converted prince had re-established his independence... (*Wounded* 6)

He criticizes R.K. Narayan and Vijay Tendulkar for their parochial views although he finds Tendulkar a little better. His India is a country in which changes have taken place. Naipaul not only criticizes concrete Indian realities but also its traditions of dance and music. So far as the Indian painting is concerned, its tradition has suffered an irrecoverable loss. The following words show Naipaul's keen insight into the various Indian arts:

> India has recovered its traditions of the classical dance, once almost extinct, and its weaving arts. But the painting tradition remains broken; painting cannot simply go back to where it left off; too much has intervened. (113)

Naipaul deplores the fact that there is no healthy tradition of democracy in India. All the democratic institutions are either borrowed or inherited from the foreign rulers. The Emergency was a sad blow to democracy in India. It hurled India once again into an era of decayed civilization. Naipaul's criticism of the Emergency is incisive:

> With the dismantling, during the Emergency, of its borrowed or inherited democratic, institutions, and with no foreign conqueror now to impose a new order, India for the first time for centuries is left alone with the blankness of its decayed civilization. (154)

Even Gandhi is not spared. Naipaul's criticism of Gandhi is severe. He says that Gandhi was made in London. He borrowed bits of his philosophy from different sources. He had no ideology of his own. He had a great following but his worshippers were often vain. Although he is worshipped in India like a god, the fact is that he was made divine by the urgency of the time. According to Naipaul there was nothing divine about him:

> Gandhi swept through India, but he has left it without an ideology. He awakened the holy land; his mahatmahood returned it to archaism; he made his worshippers vain. (146)

Naipaul criticizes Gandhi for his false concept of noble poverty. Gandhi regarded poverty as something holy and a unique possession of the Indians. This idea was against progress. Nehru was a man of progressive ideas and he did not consider poverty or complacency as something holy. He had warned the Indians against this false concept:

> Mr. Nehru had once observed that a danger in India was that poverty might be deified. Gandhianism had had that effect. The Mahatma's simplicity had appeared to make poverty holy, the

> basis of all truth, and a unique Indian possession. (38)

About Naxalism Naipaul says that it was a tragic attempt to create a revolution. The movement originated in Naxalbari in Bengal. It began in 1968. It was, by no means, a spontaneous movement. It was provoked by communists from outside India. Several landowners were killed and their land was seized. The government of the state was show in suppressing the movement. Naxalism spread like fire in several parts of India. The movement received sympathy from young men in various universities. Although Naipaul regards Naxalism as a dead movement the reality is that it has shown its presence in several new areas in India:

> They do not talk about it often; but when they do, they speak of it as a middle-class rather than a peasant-tragedy. One man put it high: he said that in the Naxalite movement India had lost the best of a whole generation, the most educated and idealistic of its young people. (79)

India: A Million Mutinies Now is the product of Naipaul's third visit to India. Scholars are of the opinion that Naipaul is a maturer writer here. Although his criticism of India continues, it becomes wiser and more balanced. The unsympathetic approach of *An Area of Darkness* and *India: A Wounded Civilization* is replaced by a desire to understand India in a better way. Shanthi Sivaraman rightly remarks:

> *India: A Million Mutinies Now*.... surprises us by its empathy and modulated attitudes towards the country. Naipaul's early attitude and later transformation become more understandable when we examine the circumstances of his life which made him an outsider wherever he went. (*Celebration* 135)

The euphoria of freedom lasted only for a short period and various unpleasant developments were noticeable very soon. These changes were shocking. Region, caste and class became prominent and they superseded national interests. Money became important and corruption became the order of the day. The first chapter of the book has been entitled "Bombay Theatre". Naipaul notices the changes and expresses his shock in these words:

> India had changed; it was not the good and stable country it had once been. In the days of the freedom movement, political workers, honouring Gandhi, had worn homespun as an emblem of sacrifice and service, their oneness with the poor. Now the politician's homespun stood for power. (*Millian* 4)

As he arrived in Bombay, he found numerous criminal minded young men at the airport. Policemen who were there did not help people properly. Naipaul felt as if there was no rule of law in India. Due to narrow selfish ends, India had become a place of numerous mutinies. Naipaul did not feel at home in India even in his third visit. He found himself no better than a refugee:

> I felt like a refugee. There was a crowd at the entrance; and criminally inclined young men ... Policemen were guarding the doorway against the young men, but they seemed not to be offering protection to people... (136)

In his third visit Naipaul realized that his earlier criticism of India was not fully justified. He found India full of energy and vitality which he had missed in his earlier observations. India provided full scope for free thought and action. In spite of its weaknesses, India remained indispensable for him. He had the satisfaction of observing India rightly. H.S.Lal observes that Naipaul's enquiry of India becomes more relevant in this book:

> This is a work of great enquiry. He wishes to correct his errors of the past observation of his homeland. He finds India a country of limitless energy and power, and a land of strong determinations. The

> book is also a realization of the writer's inadequacy to understand India in right perspective. (*Vision* 46)

Naipaul visited several places in India and met people from various walks of life. His sympathy for the minorities is obvious as he himself belongs to a minority community in Trinidad. However, the book has its own defects and it is not a complete assessment of India. He fails to understand the Indian spirituality. He lays emphasis only on physical aspects – a peculiar defect of the postmodernist writers. Purabi Panwar observes:

> Predictably, he hardly made an attempt to understand the spiritual aspect of life in India. His conversation with Papu the stockbroker, practising brahamins like Pravas and Deviah were about the ritualistic aspects of religion. This could be read as a postmodernist trait which does not recognize anything which is not physical. (*India* 132)

Naipaul is shocked to find that there have risen in India various groups which can easily be called the militant groups. They are full of fighting spirit and they have established their identity as warring groups. The rising of the Shiv Sena in Maharashtra, the D.M.K. in the south and that of Dalits under the notorious title the Panthers can be taken as examples. In the following lines Naipaul describes the 'Fort' of the Shiv Sena:

> The Sena office was a Sena fort, and there were 40 like it in Thane. In one way, it was martial make-believe; in another way, it was perfectly real. There were constant group fights in the locality. Some of the fights were between the Sena and the Dalits, ... (*Million* 26)

In south India the D.M.K. emerged as a powerful political party. The influence of national leaders like Gandhi and Nehru was hardly felt there. The D.M.K. was the product of a deep rooted Dravidian movement which had its own leaders and political ideals. Thus India was no more united politically. There were regional parties and political groups which fought for regional causes and overlooked national interests:

> The party that had won the state election in 1967 was the DMK, the Dravidian Progressive Movement. It had deep roots; it had its own prophet and its own politician - leader, men who were its equivalents of Gandhi and Nehru, ... (210)

Naipaul is critical of India but at several places he seems to acknowledge the Indian merits. He is all praise for Shankaracharya and Ram Mohan Roy for their social reforms. He praises the latter as a great modern reformer who brought new learning of Europe to India. At times he seems prejudiced against India. For example he criticizes India for its vastness. Trinidad was no bigger than Goa. India's simplicity also does not appeal to him. India appeared to him as a land of under-sized people, under-nourished animals and crumbling villages:

> ...... a landscape made monotonous by its size and frightening by its very simplicity and its special quality of exhaustion: poor choked crops in small crooked fields, under-sized people, under-nourished animals, crumbling villages and towns which, even while they develop, have an air of decay. (Mishra, *Writer* 3)

The Loss of El Dorado (1969) is Naipaul's another non-fictional work. It is different from his other non-fictional works in various ways. The book has been subtitled as *A Colonial History*. Here Naipaul attempts to formulate a history of Trinidad based on information from such sources as the British Museum, the various newspapers and public records of Trinidad. The book focuses on the colonial period in Trinidad. The first part deals with the period from 1592-1618, the second from 1633-1797 and the third from 1797-1813. Naipaul sold his home in Trinidad and shifted to England where a sense of homelessness haunted him for long. Even after writing *The Middle Passage* his quest was still incomplete. His visits to India gave him no relief and he was still in search of a home. He took to writing the present book due to economic reasons. About the significance of the title Yashoda Bhat remarks:

> *The Loss of El Dorado* was a very meaningful title. It was both a historical document as well as a metaphorical, personal, loss of a home, for thereafter, England, and not Trinidad was to be his permanent home. (*Introduction* 138)

Trinidad had undergone tremendous changes under the colonial rule. The natives of the island, the Caribs and the Amerindians had become extinct during the successive conquest of the island by England, Spain and France. Naipaul felt humiliated to think that Trinidad had no history. In fact, it had a history which had changed tremendously since its discovery by Columbus. The Indians of Columbus have been replaced by the Indians from India. In the Foreword Naipaul writes:

> It was hard to feel any wonder at the fact that, more than four hundred years after Columbus, there were Indians in a part of the world he had called the Indies; and that the people he had called Indians had vanished. (*Loss* XIII)

Although the book is a serious history, it has fictional elements within it. It is a great document of creative research. It successfully goes beyond dry fact finding. He deals with such important events as the plantation economy, the abolition of slavery, the arrival of the indentured labourers and its existence as a colony. About the peculiar mixing of various elements in the book Yashoda Bhat observes:

> Although basically a serious historical document, it has elements of fiction and it reveals Naipaul's attempt at the mingling of various literary genres

> in the postmodern style, autobiography and reportage, novel and journalism. (*Introduction* 138)

The Loss of El Dorado is a history of successive attempts by various invaders to change the destiny of Trinidad according to their own will. When the dream of El Dorado ended in smoke, the foreigners came there, not for gold but for tobacco, to continue the craze started by Releigh. The English rule was replaced by that of Spain. About the end of El Dorado adventure, Naipaul says:

> For the conquistador the El Dorado adventure ended in kidnap, solitude and lunacy. His province – the dream of the third Spanish marquisate in the New World, after Mexico and Peru – became the ghost province of the Spanish Empire. (*Loss* 3)

Naipaul narrates the history with the detachment of a scientist. There has been a long tradition of cruelty and inhuman treatment in Trinidad. Here is an example, that of Betsy Diggins. She was a cruel woman who ill-treated the few Negroes she owned. In this instance she showed cruelty towards an 'Indian' whom she did not own. She accused an Indian, a Carib from St. Vincent, of stealing some salt-fish and flour. She got some Negroes to hunt Indian down. She tied the Indian up in her yard. She tortured him unusually. The Indian cried and the cries were heard in the neighbourhood. In the morning the neighbours found him badly wounded and lying face down:

> ... two or three days later Betsy and her two Negroes, one a creole Negro, the other a new Ibo Negro, dragged the Indian down to a ravine and stoned him to death. Then Betsy herself cut up the body with a cutlass. (311)

Thus *The Loss of El Dorado* is not merely a book of history but also that of dispassionate and disinterested social criticism. It is a tribute to Trinidad which could not be his home. Naipaul immortalized Trinidad by tracing its history and bringing to light its pleasant and unpleasant social realities.

Among the Believers has been subtitled *An Islamic Journey.* It is a work of considerable length and incisive social criticism. The serious traveller delves deep into the social, political and religious realities of the four muslim countries. Naipaul laments the fact that the third world societies depend on the West for ideas. They have not succeeded in gaining cultural and intellectual independence. Kunjo Singh remarks:

> Naipaul seems unable to go beyond his *idée fixe,* the obsessive idea, of the dependence of third world societies on the West - for ideas, education, technology, everything - emphasizing their own, cultural and intellectual impoverishment. (*Reporting* 103)

He found the Iranians suffering from split personality and the Iranian society full of contradictions. He was tempted to travel the country after reading a novel by an Iranian. He found that Iran still depended on the West. The West was still indispensable for Iran. He found an almost similar situation in Pakistan. The idea of a separate nation was given in 1930 by the noted poet Sir Mohammed Iqbal. After seventeen years Pakistan became a reality but the initial euphoria subsided soon. Problems began to crop up. The flaw lay in the fact that the formation of Pakistan which must have been regarded a beginning, was mistaken for an end. The Indians who shifted to Pakistan were given the humiliating title *Mohajir.* The armed forces grabbed power and became tyrants. The situation culminated in the formation of Bangladesh. No attempt was made in Pakistan to build up new institutions and a new civilization of its own:

> Wouldn't it have been better if the creation of Pakistan had been seen as a political achievement, something to build on, rather than as a victory of the faith, something complete in itself ? ... Wouldn't

> it have been better for Muslims to trust less to the saving faith and to sit down hard-headedly to work out institutions ? (*Among* 87)

Even history is distorted. In schools the students are taught that Pakistan is a progressive nation and all evils exist outside while the reality is that Pakistan moves far and far away from progress. There is no democracy. Literary is poor. There is hardly any industrial or scientific progress. In the chapter entitled "Killing History" Naipaul gives a realistic picture of Pakistan:

> The military rule; political parties are banned. There is fifteen percent literacy, and fundamentalism stifles the universities. There is no industry, no science. The economy is a remittance economy; the emigrants, legal and illegal, pour our. (135)

The section of the book devoted to Malaysia depicts the postcolonial confusion in that country. People had lost their past and they had no definite vision of future. In big cities materialism replaced faith. Shafi is a representative of this lost generation. When he came to city from his village, he felt the onslaughts of materialism. He forgot the true nature of Islam. He was confused to the extent that he often forgot even to pray:

> Shafi said: 'When I was in the village the atmosphere is entirely different. You come out of the village. You see all the bright lights, you begin to sense the materialistic civilization around you. And I forgot about my religion and my commitments – in the sense that you had to pray. (216)

In the chapter "Brave Girls" a discussion on the difference between the rural and the urban Malaysian life is continued. There are two girls – the girl in pink and the girl in black. While the girl in pink prefers village life, the girl in black is all for city life. Naipaul reaches the conclusion that money was gaining importance and nothing could be thought about leaving money aside:

> To be Malay was to be Muslim - it was written in the laws of the new state .... Money had come to the tropical land of forest and river and village; and money created new frenzies and frustrations. (238)

In Indonesia, Naipaul had an almost similar experience. He found that people were worried about reconstructing their past. This effort led them only to confusion. There is a chapter entitled "Sitor: Reconstructing the Past". The chapter describes Naipaul's meeting with the Indonesian poet Sitor Situmorang. He was a man with a tribal background. He had lost touch with his tribal past. He suffered from a confused identity. His problem was the problem of Naipaul himself. He suffered from rootlessness:

> To some people then, especially those who towards the end of the Sukarno time could be described as 'counter - revolutionaries', he had become a figure of threat. And, as I discovered later, there were people who felt that their careers had been damaged by Sitor. (296)

Finding the Centre has been subtitled *Two Narratives.* The first narrative is "Prologue to An Autobiography". Here Naipaul traces his growth as a writer. He describes how he came to write the first page of his first book in a B.B.C. room. He was serving in the B.B.C. Caribbean service. He says that it was in England that developed a wish to be a writer as writing seemed something noble to him. At the same time he also became a colonial. He regarded himself a complete man but, when he started writing, he realized how incomplete he was. To be a writer one has to have all the facts about himself first. His writing career has been a long process of learning. In knowing himself Naipaul has known the whole world:

> To write was to learn. Beginning a book, I always felt I was in possession of all the facts about myself; at the end I was always surprised. The book before always turned out to have been written by a man with incomplete knowledge. (*Finding* 33)

Naipaul is fully aware of the fact that his approach to the world is often unduly colonial. His aim is to see life objectively but, at times, he falls into the error of being a colonial. In such moments he regards writing as a kind of display. He does not want to live in an intellectually restricted world:

> In England I was also a colonial. Out of the stresses of that, and out of my worship of the name of writer, I had without knowing it fallen into the error of thinking of writing as a kind of display. (32)

Naipaul is a historian of the world who does not believe in the significance of dates. In fact, he is a human historian and not a historian of dates. He sees things in continuity. About Chaguanas he says that it was a world for him and its history can not be divided into dates. He is a historian with a difference. His major concern is to grasp the continuous flow of humanity:

> If I read in a book that Gandhi had made his first call for civil disobedience in India in 1919, that date seemed recent. But 1919, in Chaguanas, in the life of the Indian community, was almost unimaginable. (59)

The second narrative has been entitled "The Crocodiles of Yamoussoukro". In this Naipaul studies the postcolonial conditions in the Ivory Coast. It became independent 1960 and a tribal chief took over as its first president. He developed Yamoussoukro – a small village, as a new capital of the Ivory Coast. A huge palace was built as the centre of power. As the president was a great lover of the French manners and lifestyle, he got built a French hotel. He also had a golf course to attract visitors. A great pool was dug near the palace and crocodiles were put in it. In short, the ways of the colonizers were not only continued but also improved upon. The feeding of the crocodiles was no less than a ritual as the crocodiles were sacred. A live offering especially that of a chicken marked the occasion. The crocodiles became the symbol of power which the president had inherited from the colonizers:

> This element of sacrifice, this protracted display of power and cruelty, is as unsettling as it is meant to be, and it seems to bring night and the forest close again to the dream of Yamoussoukro. (92)

Naipaul was shocked to find that independence could not bring any favourable change in the Ivory Coast. On the other hand new fears and apprehensions emerged. Independence induced a kind of anxiety regarding the future of the country. It was not clear whether the Africans would be able to establish their identity and look different from the colonizers:

> And even the success of the Ivory Coast induced a kind of anxiety. Will it last ? Will the Africans be able to take over from the French and the Israelis and the others who have built it all for them and still effectively run it ? (92)

Naipaul visited four non-Arab Muslim countries Indonesia, Iran, Pakistan and Malaysia in 1995 after a gap of sixteen years. He had visited these countries in 1979 for the first time. His first visit formed the basis of *Among the Believers*. *Beyond Belief* is the result of his second visit and it is a kind of sequel to the earlier book. Naipaul has given a Prologue to this book in which he describes that Islam outside Arab is entirely different. The Muslims of these countries are converts with an ever-changing world view. Naipaul's second visit to these countries is relevant as it underlines the changes which took place in these countries since his first visit. In the Prologue he writes:

Islam is in its origins an Arab religion. Everyone not an Arab who is a Muslim is a convert. Islam is not simply a matter of conscience or private belief. It makes imperial demands. A convert's world view alters. His holy places are in Arab lands; his sacred language is Arabic. His idea of history alters. (1)

Naipaul noticed a great change in Indonesia. Islam was getting rid of its orthodoxy and was mixing with science and political awakening. People were crazy for material prosperity although they wanted to stick to Islam firmly. In the very first chapter "The Man of the Moment" Naipaul describes Imaduddin with his changed identity. In the 70s his progressive views were discarded but now they brought him closer to power:

> The very mixture of science and Islam that had made him suspect to the authorities in the late 1970s now made him desirable, the model of the Indonesian new man, and had taken him up to the heights, had taken him very nearly to the fount of power. (7-8)

In the chapter entitled "A Convert" Naipaul narrates the story of Imaduddin's birth and upbringing. He says that the history of Indonesia is a long tale of conversion. The new and progressive approach which was taking over Islam was also a kind of conversion which was no less striking. The fundamentalists wanted to do away with their past but they were facing new challanges:

> In spite of the statesmanlike softening intention, the old Sumatran unforgivingness showed through. For the new fundamentalists of Indonesia the greatest war was to be made on their own past, and everything that linked them to their own earth. (55)

Beyond Belief is replete with social criticism of the countries Naipaul visits. He not only describes the country and the various scenes but also his encounter with various characters. He deals with the changes and how they affect Islam. Yashoda Bhat observes that the book is a rare document on Islamic Third World countries. The book bears close resemblance with *India: A Million Mutinies Now*:

> Besides descriptions of the country and the various scenes, there are lively narrations of interactions with numerous characters representing various types and through these narrations and anecdotes, emerge deep insights about the state of that country. (*Introduction* 167-8)

The section on Iran is notable for its comparison of Iran with India. Naipaul says that as a British colony, India made tremendous progress in the field of new learning. Iran remained backward and entered the twentieth century with outdated views and a heavy load of pain and nihilism:

> India, almost as soon as it became a British colony, began to be regenerated, began to receive the New Learning of Europe, to get the institutions that went with that learning ... Iran was to enter the twentieth century only with a capacity for pain and nihilism. (*Beyond* 250)

The section devoted to Pakistan shows Naipaul's insight into the history of Pakistan. He found Pakistan a troubled nation, full of various problems like those of Mohajirs and Pathans. Naipual deals with the origin of Pakistan with a rare political acumen. In the section dealing with Malaysia there is an account of Islamic missionaries spreading stories of the success of Islam.

Islam was used to create national awakening in that country.

The Writer and the World is a compilation of several pieces related to India, Africa and America. Several of these are published elsewhere also. The book is edited by Pankaj Mishra. Mishra's Introduction to the book is informative and revealing. He points out that the chief difference between Europe and the other parts of the world is that of modernity which is a reality in Europe and a dream elsewhere. India and the Caribbean share similar problems. Naipual is surprised to see both of them in their postcolonial state:

> The problems in the Caribbean were of 'manufactured societies, labour camps' that had been dependent for a very long time on empire for 'law, language, institutions, culture, even officials.' 'How, without empire, do such societies govern themselves ?' There were no easy answers. (X)

Naipaul found America entirely different. The American society was better organized and had a sound sense of security. Its political ideology was marked by a sense of national self-respect. The American society developed into a self dependent entity after the colonial period. If on the one hand it was a nation of thinkers like Norman Mailer and John Steinbeck, on the other it was a nation of power and money:

> In 1969, Naipaul also travelled to the United States; and although these essays covering Norman Mailer's mayoral campaign in New York City and John Steinbeck's Cannery Row in California describe a society much more organized and secure than the one found in the Caribbean and India... (XII)

Literary Occasions is another book edited by Pankaj Mishra with an Introduction by him. It is a collection of essays, some of which appeared elsewhere also. The Nobel Lecture by Naipaul is included in the book. In the Introduction Pankaj Mishra states that Conrad helped Naipaul understand not only his peculiar situation but also his typical state as the colonial exile. For the most part Naipaul worked in a literary tradition shaped by the colonizers. Naipaul's sense of respect and indebtedness to Conrad is obvious in his words:

It is interesting to reflect on writers' myths. With Conrad there is the imperialist myth of the man of honour, the stylist of the sea. It misses the best of Conrad, but it at least reflects the work. (180)

Naipaul's Nobel Lecture has been given the title "Two Worlds". In fact, these two worlds are the one within himself and the other outside. Both of these worlds are full of confusion and clash. It is this clash which makes Naipaul a serious traveller. In his speech Naipaul said that he himself is the subject of his books. He goes through the world as an observer. He continues to revise his views on the world. This process began very early in his life. It was as a child that he realized the existence of two worlds:

> So as a child I had this sense of two worlds, the world outside that tall corrugated-iron gate, and the world at home - or, at any rate, the world of my grandmother's house. It was a remnant of our caste sense, the thing that excluded and shut out. (187)

A Writer's People is a book of random views on different persons and places. Writers, politicians and social workers are put to severe criticism. Naipaul is unsparing even with the great figures like Mahatma Gandhi and Vinoba Bhave. Naipaul regarded Anthony Powell as a great novelist but when he went through his works he found that he was not flawless. In the following lines Naipaul critisises him for his lack of interest in the English social life.

There is a kind of writing that undermines its subject. Most good writing, I believe, is like that. *A View to a Death*, for all its care in the delineation of county manners, leaves English social life just where the writer found it. And the same is true of *The Music of Time*. (40)

Naipaul holds the view that there was nothing great about Gandhi and his philosophy. He gathered bits of his philosophy in London and Africa. About Vinoba Bhave he says that he was a foolish follower of Gandhi. He wished to become a Mahatma but his attempt was futile as he was in the grip of mental idleness which had entered his soul. The following words are notable for the scathing criticism of the Acharya:

> There was a foolish man, Vinoba Bhave, who in the early 1950s tried to do a Gandhi repeat. He had been brought up in Gandhi's various ashrams. The mental idleness of those places had softened his brain and entered what might be called his soul. (172)

Even Nirad C. Chaudhuri is not spared. Naipaul goes to the extent of saying that he was not a scholar. His *Autobiography* is not so great a book as it has been estimated by various critics. Only a few parts of the book are scholarly. When Naipaul went through the book, he felt the same kind of disillusionment he had felt on reading Powell's works. Chaudhuri may be a scholar for many but he is a pseudo-scholar for Naipaul:

> Chaudhuri, in spite of all the great names he takes, was not a scholar. He had no idea what scholarship meant. He held on to the idea only because it was the main part of his self-esteem. (188)

However, Naipaul is not always critical. He never fails to notice the merits of persons and places. Although he criticizes Gandhi for his flaws, he clearly mentions that he was a man of rare qualities. He was a sage or saint. He was humble but not weak, soft-spoken but not docile. Even those who disagreed with him acknowledged his merits:

> His physical description of Gandhi at this stage is fascinating. It complements Huxley's portrait of a few years later. It shows the steel that was in the bare-backed sage or saint. The eyes were mild and 'deep', bright with energy and determination. He was humble but precise and hard ... (117)

Naipaul's criticism of the world is unique of its kind. The autobiographical element is clearly perceptible but it never hampers Naipaul's disinterestedness. He is an ethnographer a sociologist, anthropologist and, above all, a historian. His travel writing combines these elements in a unique way. He is an observer of the world who sees it from various angles and points of view. He can safely be called the pioneer of the new kind of travel writing. Yashoda Bhat observes:

> Of late, a new concept of travel writing has come into vogue. Travelogues seem to become a blend of history, ethnography, anthropology or sociology and autobiography. Travel writing is now passing through a phase of 'generic crossroads.' (*Introduction* 108)

Naipaul's travels to the Caribbean islands, India, Iran, Pakistan, Africa, America, Malaysia and Indonesia have yielded relevant criticism of the societies based on Naipaul's vision of the people of different parts of the world. His criticism shows his knowledge of men and manners, cultures and civilizations. He has created a corpus of valuable social criticism which will continue to retain significance in future. Mallikarjun Patil observes in his article "Naipaul, V.S.: The Travel-Writer":

> His travelogues depict the life he has seen in different parts of the world. The vivid accounts he narrates in the books also display Naipaul's knowledge of men and manners, culture and civilized or uncivilized way of life he has beholden. (145)

Naipaul is basically a journalist and his journalistic style is marked by objectivity. This objectivity of style has helped him a great deal in criticizing the world in dispassionate manner. His style has developed consistently since the beginning of his career but it has successfully retained its objectivity. In short, his style is suited to his purpose. Rafe Dalleo observes in the article "The World, The Text, The Caribbean Writer: Representation in the Work of V.S. Naipaul":

> V.S. Naipaul's writing has always kept moving, searching for new forms, structures and style to better represent the world. After he had seemingly, settled on a journalistic, 'objective' style during the late 1960s and 1970s .... (14)

Naipaul is not without demerits. Critics have blamed him for his imperialistic bias and personal prejudices. His ignorance is also clearly perceptible at various places. But the fact remains that his non-fiction brings to the reader the reality in its most naked form. These works not only convey the truth but also make interesting reading. Herein lies the greatness of the serious traveller - V.S. Naipaul. Yashoda Bhat rightly mentions:

> There may be imperialistic biases, personal prejudices, ignorant views in a whirlwind tour but also some fresh insights. On the whole, a rare and interesting and even a controversial view, but an authentic one making interesting and meaningful reading. (*Introduction* 134)

3

The Society-Individual Relationship

V.S. Naipaul not only criticizes the world at large but also examines the relationship existing between individual and society. Every individual is the product of his society and the worth of his being depends on how much he contributes to his society. Naipaul traces his own identity in his works. He probes the forces which compelled him to become a writer. He has lived in different societies and his personality as a writer bears the clear marks of each of them. In fact, it is his major concern to find out his growth as an individual. He carries out this search through various characters in his works. Pankaj Mishra observes:

> To recognize the fragmented aspects of your identity; to see how they enable you to become who you are; to understand what was necessary about a painful and awkward past and to accept it as part of your being - this ceaseless process ... is what much of Naipaul's work has been compulsively engaged in. (*Occasions* XVI)

Naipaul was born in Trinidad in a Hindu family of Indian descent. His ancestors were taken to Trinidad from India by the Britishers as indentured labourers. These

Indians became a part and parcel of the Trinidadian society. They engaged in several occupations. Some of them contributed to the literature of that country also. Naipaul's father was a writer of considerable reputation. Naipaul had literature in his blood right from his early childhood. About the contribution of the Indians to the Trinidadian life Yashoda Bhat remarks:

> Although these Indians lived isolated lives, they soon got integrated on several layers and became indispensable for the development of Trinidad. They also contributed to the literature of the area and the Naipaul family is an outstanding example of it. (*Introduction* 19)

Naipaul was an early victim of rootlessness and displacement. Expatriate literature has been a rich body of literature. Terry Egleton observes that the English literature has been dominated by foreign writers like Conrad, James, Eliot, Pound, Yeats and Joyce. Naipaul's name can safely be added to these writers. When he shifted to England his early experiences got mixed with his new perceptions and this interaction yielded a rich corpus of literature. Thus, Naipaul is a product of the societies of India, Trinidad and England. His experiences of the world have added an extra charm to his writing. Bhat observes:

> Terry Egleton in his book *Exiles and Emigres* observes that the heights of English literature have been dominated by foreigners and émigrés: Conrad, James, Eliot, Pound, Yeats, Joyce ... (54)

The role of Trinidad in Naipaul's life can not be overlooked. It was in Trinidad that he developed a curiosity to know the world and the ambition to become a writer. He was inspired by his father who was journalist. His father also wished to be a writer but his career was thwarted by his early death. Journalism was an unusual occupation for an Indian of his generation living in Trinidad. It was a kind of adventure which inspired

Naipaul to take up the adventurous career of a writer. In the first part of *Finding the Centre* entitled "Prologue to an Autobiography" Naipaul writes:

> The ambition to be a writer was given me by my father. He was a journalist for much of his working life. This was an unusual occupation for a Trinidad Indian of his generation. (33)

But Trinidad could not become a fit background for Naipaul. It did not allow full scope to his mental faculties. It was a small colony which was more fit for agriculture than for intellectual activity. Naipual has stated time and again that the West provides full freedom and scope for intellectual work. It was in the B.B.C. Caribbean Service that he became a freelance journalist and a writer. The British setting was best suited to his ambition of being a writer:

> And there was my own presence in England, writing: the career wasn't possible in Trinidad, a small, mainly agricultural colony: my vision of the world couldn't exclude that important fact. (33)

Although Naipaul has the Indian blood in his veins, he is not unduly symphetic towards India. He is a neutral observer of India. In fact, it is this sense of detachment which has made him an observer of the world. Now he can not be said to belong to any nation. The Indian society shaped his individuality by creating in him a sense of disillusionment. His greatness lies in his detached approach to his background. Nanda Kishore Mishra observes:

> Such a set of mentality instead of being condemned by critics ought to be appreciated with a sort of reformative zeal. Are we not at times, in reality, vexed with some of our irrational beliefs and practice, which have lost their symbolic significance for our present day mentality ? (*Trajectory* 151)

When Naipaul came to India in search of his roots,

he found only dust and poverty. He went to the village of the Dubes but he could not find any trace of his ancestors there. His stay in India created in him a sense of 'separateness'. This sense was so great that when he left the village he did not feel like waving. In the following words he says how he was compelled to fly from his motherland:

> We drove off. I did not wave. The headlamps of the jeep shot two separate beams into the day's slowly settling dust which, made turbulent again by our passage, blotted out the scattered lights of the village. So it ended, in futility and impatience, a gratuitous act of cruelty, self-reproach and flight. (*Darkness* 286)

Naipaul's criticism of India and adoration of the West continues in *India: A Wounded Civilisation*. Naipual continues to hold the opinion that the present day India is made by the West. Even Gandhi was made in London. Indians have a false sense of history and they swallow their past blindly. Gandhi was the need of the hour. There was nothing original about his philosophy. Naipual underlines the fact that the Indian society is not fit for the full growth of its individuals. Men of achievements are made in the West which provides impetus to their growth. Nehru, the architect of modern India was shaped in England. His greatness is due to the fact that even there he was aware of his Indianness:

> In his autobiography Nehru says he was infected by the prevailing, and fashionable, anti-Semitism at Harrow School; he could hardly have failed there to have become aware of his Indianness. (*Wounded* 145)

Vinoba Bhave tried to follow the footsteps of Gandhi but failed. Naipaul thinks that the Indian society did not need another Mahatma. It is the society which creates the individual. On particular moments there is urgent need for certain kinds of individuals. Bhave tried to repeat the example of Gandhi but the Indian society rejected him. His spirituality was old and outdated, and his ideas retrograde:

> Bhave, in the vanity of his spiritual perfection, is more than a decadent Gandhian. His religion is a kind of barbarism; it would return men to bush. It is the religion of poverty and dust. And it is not extra-ordinary that Bhave's ideas about education should be like those of Mr. Squeers. (149)

His third book on India *India: A Million Mutinies Now* is an still improved assessment of India. Critics have expressed this opinion almost unanimously and frequently that Naipaul's understanding of and sympathy for India developed by degrees. In this book he presents a wider picture of India through various characters. He found India becoming a better nation everyday. It was gaining new vitality and it was no more a nation with only a glorious past. Its bright future was ensured by the fact that it was gaining the ability to use the skills of its people:

> Naipaul has projected through his characters a large vision of India, an India with a human association rather than a clanish, casteist obligation, an India which will utilise all 'the bravery and the skills of its people' ... (Sivaraman, *Celebration* 137)

Due to this vitality, India could gain independence. After independence there came an era of euphoria. This euphoria was later replaced by a million small fights. Naipaul sees nothing wrong in these fights. He thinks that they are a sign of a new kind of awakening. They indicate to the fact that India is heading towards a new intellectual life. Shanthi Sivaraman goes on to say:

> India is now a land of a million little mutinies – 'supported by twenty kind of group excess, sectarian excess, religious excess.' Naipaul sees

> these excesses as the beginnings of self-awareness, the beginning of an intellectual life ... (138)

Naipaul meets various persons and visits various places to revise his earlier impressions of India. He meets Mr. Patil, Mr. Roate and Mr. Ghate, and Ambedkar's followers. He visits Madras, Calcutta, Lucknow, Delhi and the Punjab. These experiences give him a fresh insight into the new Indian conditions which he records in *India: A Million Mutinies Now*. Mallikarjun Patil considers the book as a splendid work which records the changes and developments in India:

> Indeed, whatever the Indian critics think of Naipaul's other travelogues on India, his *India: A Million Mutinies Now* is a splendid work about changes and developments in India ... No doubt those who want to know India and Naipaul, must read the book. (*India* 265)

While in Maharastra the Shiv Sena grew as a considerable force, in the Punjab Bhindranwale turned from a preacher to a politician. These were the products of typical social conditions. Describing Mr. Ghate Naipaul writes that he was born in a chawl. When he became a political force he had options to go to better places. But he stayed in the chawl as it was of political advantage for him. Naipaul describes how individuals are given a typical shape by their societies:

> And people could be made by the conditions in which they lived. As animals could be made by the conditions in which they were reared ... So people who lived in the little spaces of Bombay dwellings got used to those spaces ... (*Million* 60)

In the Punjab a movement was raised to establish a separate Khalistan. Bhindranwale, who was a preacher, was forced to become a warrior by the conditions in which he was placed. Although the movement could not achieve its goal, it became a noted event in the Indian history.

In the following words Naipaul describes Bhindranwale's changing roles:

> Bhindrawale came to the sanctuary of the Golden Temple in 1982, and he turned it into his fortress and domain. He was thirty-five. Four years before, he had been only a preacher and the head of a Sikh seminary; now he was a politician and a warrior. (446)

Naipaul's writings, specially his travelogues, have been severely criticized for their unsparing and ruthless criticism of the world. But the fact is that Naipaul is with his own redeeming factors. He is free from doctrines and religious influences which hamper an objective assessment of the world. No institution, person or book, can mislead him. He examines the varying relations of individual and society in several parts of the world. Bijay Kumar Das observes about Naipaul's travelogues in his article "The Question of identity: A Note on V.S. Naipaul's Travel Writing on India and Trinidad":

> ... they have redeeming features. ... Naipaul seems to awe allegiance to no institution, to no doctrine and to no religion. He spares none. His commitment is to his own vision of life whatever it may be. (160)

Naipaul observes that India had been a land of rebellians in the past. After independence several groups emerged and almost every individual stuck to one or the other. There was no cause after independence for which the Indians could fight as a united country. These groups have their own leaders and chieftains who wished to gain power and popularity. Each one of them wanted to be great as Buddha or Nanak:

> People within the Hindu fold had always been rebelling against Brahmin orthodoxy, Vishwa Nath had said; and everyone who had rebelled had started a sect with its own rigidities. Buddha had

> rebelled; Guru Nanak, the first Guru of the Sikhs, had rebelled. (*Million* 421)

Naipaul's study of various societies continues in his two journeys to four non-Arab Islamic countries. *Among the Believers* and *Beyond Belief* are the valuable fruits of these journeys. Naipaul's account of these journeys is informative as well as highly interesting. He notices not only the features of the landscape but also the characteristics of the people. He examines how these societies treat their individuals. Characters like Behzad, Sitor Situmorang, Shafi, Nusrat, Ahmed, Prasojo and Masood help Naipaul in carrying out his study. The autobiographical note adds an extra charm. Kunjo Singh observes about *Among the Believers*:

> In spite of its being a work of considerable length *Among the Believers*, has title that goes beyond the initial observation about dependence made in chapter one, as far as general comment on the societies of these Islamic countries is concerned. (*Reporting* 103)

In the chapter "The Night Train from Mashhad" Naipaul describes the features of Behzad's personality. He is a young man brought up in Shia culture. He has a passion for revolution and this revolution is not separated from his faith. He takes many things granted. He has Communist bent of mind. He thinks that there is no true freedom in the West. Naipaul is surprised to think how different Behzad is from him:

> He had no religious faith. But he had grown up in Shia Iran, and his idea of justice for the pure and the suffering was inseparable from the idea of punishment for the wicked. His dream of the reign of Stalin was a version of the dream of the rule of Ali - the Prophet's true successor. (60)

What Naipaul notices is that while the Muslims stick firmly to their faith, they want the material prosperity of the West. They criticize the West for its ideology but they wish to adopt its technology. They dislike the social and moral values prevailing in the West but they are all praise for the worldy achievements of the West. Yashoda Bhat subscribes to this view. She illustrates the point by making a distinction between culture and technology:

> The contradiction that Muslims emotionally reject western civilization but they also need it and stick to it can also be viewed with a different perspective. This can be explained by making a distinction between culture and technology. (*Introduction* 126)

When Naipaul went to Pakistan he found things entirely different. Iran was the land of oil and money while Pakistan was one of desert and poverty. With almost double population, Pakistan had only a small portion of Iran's income. Iran earned millions through oil export. Pakistan could manage a meagre income through the export of rice, leather and cotton. With all this the noticeable thing was that in Pakistan Islam was more of a policy than a faith:

> Iqbal's argument was like this. Islam is not only an ethical ideal, it is also 'a certain kind of polity'. Religion for a Muslim is not a matter of private conscience or private practice, as Christianity can be for the man in Europe. (*Among* 85)

The section devoted to Malaysia deals with the changes taking place in that country and how they affect the individuals. There is Shafi who has left his village and come to the city. It seems to him as if he has moved out of the paradise in which he was happily placed. The move has expelled him from his heaven. There is the Tamil driver who feels the same kind of loss. In the postcolonial Malaysia there are several individuals like these. They are the lost men who have a constant sense of disturbance with them. They find it difficult to cope with the new changes:

> Shafi worked for the Muslim cause. He didn't wear Arab cloths. But he understood the young men who did. Shafi had come to Kuala Lumpur from a village in the north. The disturbance of the move was still with him. (216)

The changes in Malaysia were inevitable. Even men like Shafi who felt that the village ways were the true Malay ways realized that the old ways had to be changed. The old puritan views could not stand the test of time. A new kind of openness was the need of the hour. Naipaul marked a change in Shafi's views during his stay in Malaysia. Shafi represented a whole class which shared a similar opinion:

> It was what Shafi had told me: that contradiction in Shafi's thought had come out towards the end of our last conversation. The village way was the true Malay way; but that way had to be altered. Belief had to be purified, the old pagan traditions of the village uprooted. (252)

In Indonesia, Naipaul found a different scene. Indonesia had a unique past. Islam came there in the fifteenth century. Before this there was the Hindu - Buddhist culture. The traits of this old culture were still to be found there although the culture had erased itself almost completely. In Malaysia true Islam was to be found only in the countryside. In Indonesia the uniqueness of civilization prevailed everywhere. It was this civilization which created the strong man Sukarno. About this special feature of the Indonesian culture, Naipaul writes:

> Indonesia, like Malaysia, was a Muslim country. But the pre-Islamic past, that in Malaysia seemed to be only a matter of village customs, in Indonesia - or Java - showed as a great civilization. Islam, which had come only in the fifteenth century, was the formal faith. (279)

In Indonesia, there was a strange fusion of the present Islamic culture and the Hindu past. Old mythological names from the great Hindu epics were no more Hindu names. They had Islamic significance. The five pandavas stood for five different Islamic notions. Parsojo is a typical product of this strange fusion. It makes him a little mysterious. He is a Muslim but with a difference. Naipaul describes him thus:

> .... the story he was telling me came from the ancient Hindu epic of the *Mahabharata,* which had lived in Java for 1400 years, had taken Javanese roots, and had then been adapted to Islam. Prasojo, a Javanese and a Muslim, lived with beautiful mysteries. Scholarship, applied to his past, would have undermined what had become his faith, his staff. (299)

A follow-up to *Among the Believers* is *Beyond Belief* in which Naipaul explores what Islam has done to the histories of the four non-Arab Muslim countries he had visited seventeen years back and which he now visits again. The book is dedicated to Nadira Khannun Alvi. Divided into four sections the book takes up Indonesia first. Naipaul meets Imaduddin after seventeen years. He narrates the story of a scientist who builds N-250. He is not only a scientist but also a Muslim leader. Due to his conflict with Suharto he was put to jail. He is very close to Habibie the minister for research and technology. Habibie's ambition was that Indonesia must have its own aeroplanes. Through this he wished to create an Indonesian industrial revolution:

> The idea behind the idea - as I had read in some newspapers - was that such a venture wouldn't only deliver aeroplanes. It would also give many thousands of people a high and varied technological training; out of this would come an Indonesian industrial revolution. (*Beyond* 8)

Naipaul explores how the converted people view their past. Conversion is a major phenomenon in Indonesia. There is a chapter "A Convert" in this section. In this Naipaul describes the conversion of an American (an Oklahoman) to Islam. Everyone present at the ceremony is full of joy. Imaduddin gives him a new name Mohammad Adam Khalid. He welcomes him back to Islam. In his view conversion is nothing but coming back to Islam. According to him Islam means conversion:

> When the chanting ended, Imaduddin, smiling at the Oklahoman, said to him in English, 'We welcome you back to Islam. Back to Islam, because in our belief everyone was born as a Muslim, without sin. You have come back to Islam because you have opened your heart to the truth. (50)

When Naipaul visited Iran for the second time he discovered that religion had become a tyranny. It was as oppressive as the secularism of the Shah. Naipaul describes the case of Mr. Jaffrey. He was an Indian who first shifted to Pakistan and then to Iran. As he was a man with the Indian - British background he found himself uneasy and restless both in Pakistan and in Iran. He had ideas of democracy and law which could not flourish in these settings. Owing to his discomfiture he confined himself to the reporters' room. His case illustrates how societies oppress individuals:

> But it was just at this point that Mr. Jaffrey's Indian - British education and experience came into play, ideas of democracy and law and institutions, the separation of church and state, ideas that made him sit at his typewriter in the reporters' room ... (155)

At the same time there are individuals who do not lose heart. Ali's case is an example of this. He made his fortune and was comfortably placed. But instead of being complacent he became more full of revolutionary zeal. He wanted freedom based on faith. Ali is different from Jaffrey as he is not an odd man in Iran.

He said, 'We expected a revolution based on heavenly laws and laws of nature.' Heavenly laws it was like his own version of Mr. Jaffrey's *jame towhidi,* and Arash's search for the justice of Ali - Ali the fourth caliph, the Shia Hero - saint. (176)

The idea of a separate Pakistan was conveyed in a concrete way in 1930 by the famous poet Mohammed Iqbal and this idea became a reality in 1947. Pakistan came into existence but its future was uncertain. This uncertainty became more horrible day by day as Pakistan could not move in the right direction. Religious fundamentalism made people narrow minded. Only those could keep their minds open who went out to gain education and progress. Shahbaz is one such character. In the chapter "Guerilla" Naipaul describes him thus:

> It was said in Pakistan that Pakistanis, because of their uncertainty in the wider world, always tried to bring their fellows down. Shahbaz wasn't like that; he readily offered admiration to Pakistanis as well as to other people. (301)

There is another character who is entirely different from Shahbaz. It is Salman. After partition there was created a strong anti-India sentiment in Pakistan. This sentiment was aggravated by religious fanaticism. Fight against India was considered as part of *jihad*. The idea of *jihad* was so fascinating that it attracted almost every youth in Pakistan. Salman was also captivated by this idea. He wished to sacrifice his life for the holy war against non-Muslims and specially against India:

> In this way Salman was introduced to the idea of *jihad,* holy war. It was a special Muslim idea. He explained it like this: 'In Christianity Christ died for all Christians. He can ensure heaven for them. In Islam Mohammed can only make a submission in your favour for being a follower of his. (327)

The section on Malaysia comes last in the book. Naipaul gives an account of Islamic missionaries spreading stories of the success of Islam. In Malaysia there was a strong sense that the Chinese cheated the nation out of its peace and complacency. Islamic sentiments were used to wake up the Muslim youth movement. Shafi becomes a strong believer under the influence of the Islamic missionaries. Earlier these missionaries were busy in Iran and Pakistan but now they focused their attention on Malaysia:

> ... in 1979 Islam was being made to carry that general rage. Malays of Shafi's generation had become passionate believers: and their belief was given edge by Islamic missionaries, who were especially busy in 1979, with the revolution in Iran and the Islamising terror of General Zia in Pakistan. (386)

While some societies make individuals revolutionary and even fanatic, some others make them writers and thinkers. In *A Writer's People* Naipaul traces the growth of several eminent writers. He describes three writers who got their material and inspiration from the Caribbean background. They are Edgar Mittelholzer, Samuel Selvon, and Naipaul's own father. Edgar was born in Guyana. He spent a hard and wandering early life. His experiences are reflected in his novel *A Morning in the Office*. Samuel Selvon was a Trinidadian with the Indian background. His novel *A Brighter Sun* is based on his wartime experiences. So far as his own father's case is concerned he became a writer to depict the condition of transplanted people and to reconstruct the societies they had left behind. Thus the Caribbean and the Indian societies created writers of great merit. About his own father Naipaul writes:

> He is possibly the first writer of the Indian diaspora, the first to write of its transplanted people, unprotected peasants, seeking as if by a necessary instinct to recreate the society they left behind, and to a large extent succeeding. (*Writer's* 31)

According to Naipaul it is not easy to become a writer. For this, one has to have vision and the right way of seeing and feeling. He finds faults with the Indian as well as the English way of seeing things. He says that there are writers who have earned name but who are not without defects. Anthony Powell and Nirad C. Chaudhuri are such writers. About Powell he says that he held him in high esteem and cherished his friendship but when he went through his works he was shocked to find that Powell was, in fact, a man of defective vision:

> When I was free I settled down to read. I got two of the paperback omnibus volumes, and read six connected books from the middle. I was appalled. Powell had had a little American success with one book, and I felt that this perhaps had corrupted him. (37)

About Chaudhuri Naipaul says that he is incapable of analysis. As soon as he attempts it, he becomes wordy and vain. His *Autobiography* is generally considered a great book but its final impression is one of a shallow work. Naipaul finds that, in fact, it is the fault of the Indian way of seeing things. Indians look but they do not see. Chaudhuri does not care for the patience of the readers. The result is that the so-called great literary work has failed to attract readers:

> As soon as Chaudhuri attempts analysis he becomes vain and mad and begins to use too many words, indifferent to the reader's patience. So it happens that out of a strange, suicidal vanity his once solid book ends in the air, and its better parts have lacked readers. (183)

The Writer and the World deals with the Indian, the African and the American occasions Naipaul studies India from different angles. In Calcutta he finds the confrontation of the East and the West most striking. Almost every individual is under the spell of the Western education and civilization. They are proud of being the true followers of the British rulers. They not only adopt the Western ways of living but also their mode of thinking. In this respect Calcutta is different from the other three big cities developed by the Britishers:

> When he joins his firm his first name is changed. The Indian name of Anand, for example, might become Andy; Dhandeva will become Danny, Firdaus Freddy, Jamshed Jimmy. Where the Indian name cannot be adapted, the box-wallah will most usually be known as Bunty. (*Writer* 13)

Describing and election scene in Ajmer, Naipaul gives a glimpse of the Indian politicians. These politicians have no ideology and sense of ethics. They do not discriminate between good and bad, moral and immoral. There is Bishweshwar who contests election against his own uncle and godfather Mukut. He is a handsome fellow with nothing else but politics to do. If politics is taken away from him, he is left with only poverty and starvation. The Indian politicians have hardly taken any lesson from their British predecessors:

> Mr. Bishweshwar was as tall and plump as a film star. He was a post-independence politician, an organization man. People in his own party said of him: 'Politics is his profession.' And: 'If politics were taken away from him he would hardly be having two square meals a day.' (37)

Naipaul deals with not only politicians but also with peasants and tribals. In fact, he has a greater sympathy for the latter as he thinks that they have been swallowed up by 'histories'. These are men who find no place in academic and journalistic records of Africa and Asia. They are caught in the postcolonial confusion. They have lost their past in their turbulent present. Their heroism lies in their ceaseless fight for their dignity. Naipaul seems to share this fight for individual dignity. For him these individuals are more important than the ideologies which work upon them and confuse them. Pankaj Mishra observes in the Introduction to the book:

> . The individuals these ideologies work upon are usually absent from academic and journalistic accounts of African and Asian countries. But in Naipaul's essays, they stand very clearly, in the midst of the chaos and pain of their underdeveloped societies, and 'awakening to ideas, history, a knowledge of injustice and a sense of their own dignity.' (XIV)

Naipaul's experiences are multi-layered. They create in him pain and anguish. The deprivation of Trinidad and the misery of India leave him agonized. But these experiences never end in bleak pessimism. The lost glory and the present deception do not confound his faith in human perfectibility. He carries within himself various visions of the world. These visions may be clashing but they can not hurl him into depression and hopelessness. In recognizing the dignity of the individual, Naipaul confirms his own dignity:

> But what's more remarkable is that Naipaul's acute sense of lost glory and contentment, his anguished perception of deception and tragedy - things inseparable from his background and experience - co-exist with an attitude of acceptance and optimism, with a well-founded faith in human striving and perfectibility. (XV)

"East Indian" is a revealing article collected in the *Literary Occasions* edited by Pankaj Mishra. In this Naipaul discusses how the Indians living in the Caribbean setting have changed from the original. Their languages have changed. Rituals have undergone striking changes Hindus are buried as open air cremation is forbidden by the Health Authorities. They try to stick to traditions but their changed setting forces them to undergo changes. Naipaul is caught in the crisis of identity. He is an Indian but to be so is not easy for him. Naipaul's case illustrates how an individual is affected by the social conditions in which he is placed:

> East Indians, British Indians, Hindustanis. But the West Indies are part of the New World and these Indians of Trinidad are no longer of Asia. The temples and mosques exist and appear genuine. But the languages that came with them have decayed. (40)

Naipaul is of the firm opinion that a writer's sensibilities are shaped by his society. It often forces him to choose a particular literary form. Naipaul examines the writing of Kipling, Gandhi, Nirad C. Chaudhuri, Conrad and R.K. Narayan in *The Writer and the World*. He comes to the conclusion that they were compelled to write because of their respective social conditions. These writers owe their virtues and vices to their societies. Naipaul himself became a writer under typical social conditions. His Indian past compelled him to write. His Caribbean and British experiences inspired him to explore the world. Pankaj Mishra observes in the Introduction to *Literary Occasions*:

> They depend on particular, often highly original, interpretations of history and invariably turn upon the problems of self-definition: how writers incarnate or reject the deeper assumptions of the societies they belong to and write about; how their chosen literary form reflects or distorts their particular experiences of the world. (XII)

Naipaul had the privilege of living in different continents and studying the society - individual relationship in different settings. Some critics think that Naipaul grew cynical towards these societies but the fact is that he was less cynical than Gao Xingjian, his predecessor in receiving the Nobel Prize. Naipaul was in a state of voluntary exile throughout these journeys. He was always detached and at a distance everywhere. This typical position enabled him to study his own self as well as individuals like him. Nanda Kishore Mishra observes in the article "Trajectory of Displacement: Expatriate Sensibility of V.S. Naipaul":

> The account of his expatriate experience, his self-portraiture reveals the pain of his displacement; at the same time makes him cynical about other races and cultures including that of India. But as an expatriate his life is less traumatic than Gao Xingjian, the noted Chinese author who won the most prestigious Nobel Prize for literature in 2000. (147)

Naipaul underlines the fact that mahatmas, writers, thinkers, prophets, fanatics and mutineers are the products of the varied social conditions. The influence of society is so overwhelming that none can escape it. Even those who break new grounds are the products of society. The forces shape the individual according to the requirements of the society. The individual differences also matter. Sometimes the same social conditions create varied personalities. The society-individual relationship varies from place to place and from person to person. Naipaul had the vantage ground for growing as a writer. About the unique position of Naipaul as a writer Mishra goes on to say:

> Naipaul possesses all the advantages of portraying the cross-cultural relations in the postcolonial era. From a study of his writings one can gather that Naipaul never suffered from any anxiety of outside influence. He has no alternative community to identify himself. This unique position makes him a neutral observer. (148)

In his works Naipaul deals with the theme of homelessness in his own style. He read many writers and critics think that his style is close to that of Joseph Conrad, but the fact is that his style is entirely his own. The influence of great writers like Dickens, Conrad, Swift, Dryden and Shakespeare may be traced but the originality of his approach is intact. According to Naipaul the influence of others only hinders a writer's originality. Lakshmi Kumari Sharma points out:

> ... he admits to have read Dickens, Charlotte, Bronte, Conrad, Swift, Dryden and Shakespeare and he finally comes to the conclusion that they, instead of giving inspiration to write, make it difficult for him to be fair to the society around him. (*Man* 28-29)

4

Religion in Modern Times

Naipaul is a great explorer of the world and, in the process of his exploration, he has constantly kept an eye on the role of religion in various societies. As a child, he saw India scattered about him in physical objects - drums, mats, brass vessels and all the paraphernalia of the prayer room. He was aware of his Hindu background but he was first a detached observer of everything, including religion, and then a Hindu. He was never interested in rituals. Later, when he travelled throughout the world he continued his neutral observations. He was never at home in any religion or religious group. Yashoda Bhat describes his approach to religion in these words:

> He states that he was never interested in the religious rituals and other details and whatever experiences he had, had been passed on to him by the members of his large joint family amidst whom he lived. (*Introduction* 123)

Naipaul's works are marked by a deep sense of disillusionment with India. He came to India in search of his roots but he found only disillusionment in the country of his ancestors. The Hindu rituals and places of worship held no attraction for him. His writings show that he is not at all sentimental about the past and at the same time he has no love for the country of his birth or origin. Namrata Rathore Mahanta remarks:

> India shocked Naipaul because it challenged his idea of himself. The contradiction between the imagined India of Trinidad and the actual country was too overwhelming to be confronted. The only immediate solution available was that of escape. (*Trilogy* 27)

In his Indian trilogy he describes various occasions when he found Hinduism more mysterious than real. In *An Area of Darkness* he describes his pilgrimage to the Cave of Amarnath. He was encouraged by Karan Singh, the Maharaja of Kashmir to undertake the pilgrimage. He is curious about the discovery of the Cave and the formation of its mystery without bothering too much about its religious significance. He found the Cave a mystery like Delphi. About Hinduism he remarks that it is scarcely a religion. His detached observation of Hinduism is embodied in these words:

> It was a mystery, like Delphi, of the older world. It had survived because it was of India and Hinduism which, without beginning, without end, scarcely a religion, continued as a repository and living record of man's religious consciousness. (*Darkness* 164)

The journey to the Cave was mismanaged. They had to camp at various places and, at one such place, Naipaul found every pilgrim defecating in the open. He could not find a clean place to wash himself. There were sadhus from all corners of the country and they formed a big crowd. They were fed by the Kashmir government. The arrangement was supervised by Tourist Department. All the pilgrims were 'tourists-cum-pilgrims'. Naipaul describes his experience of the journey dispassionaely in these words:

> The camping ground, when we got to it, was crowded; the rocky banks of the turbulent mountain river were already lined with defecating pilgrims, and soon it would have been difficult to find an accessible washing spot that was unsullied. (171)

Naipaul is sad to notice that the Indians are ignorant of their glorious past. They do not realize the glory of their religion. Their knowledge of the past does not go beyond their grandfathers. The Indians live in a state of darkness and they feel complacent there. Indians must develop a greater awareness of themselves, their religion and culture. Colon observes in this context:

> V.S. Naipaul said that ignorance of the Indian community permeates inside as well as outside of itself. Indians must learn more about themselves. They must learn about the constituents of their community and of their culture. (*Memory* 167)

India is full of differences of various kinds. In the North, people consider themselves as the descendents of the Aryans. In the South, the black Indians are known as Dravidians. All of them are the followers of Hinduism but even this similarity has failed to eliminate the Aryan-Dravidian difference. Naipaul considers it as the failure of religion:

> You must read some of the old Hindu books. They will tell you. In those days it was unclean to kiss a very black woman on the lips. You think this is just a crazy Sikh talking ? You read. This Aryan-Dravidian business isn't new. And it's starting up again. (*Darkness* 247)

In India, temples are the symbols of magic and mystry. Several of them are declared national monuments. In *India: A Wounded Civilization* Naipaul describes the temple of Vijayanagar. It is a temple with clusters of musical stone columns that can still be played. The temple has been declared a national monument by the Archaeological

Department. The pilgrims go to the temple as they think that it is the magic of God which has saved it from destruction for centuries. They do not go deep into its religious significance:

> To the pilgrims Vijayanagar is its surviving temple. The surrounding destruction is like proof of the virtue of old magic; just as the fantasy of past splendour is accommodated within an acceptance of present squalor. (*Wounded* 5)

Naipaul is an objective observer of his own faith. He is never swayed by false romanticism. His understanding of India and Hinduism may not be perfect but his treatment of them is objective and unsparing. The fact is that the Indian culture and civilization are so complex that it is not easy to present a perfectly accurate account of them. Yashoda Bhat holds a similar opinion:

> Naipaul's position vis-à-vis India is a special one. But these or similar difficulties are also experienced by several people new to India and is because the culture and civilization of India are complex because of its ancient history and the varied forces which moulded it. (*Naipaul* 122)

During his study of India Naipaul found that it is a land of multiple religious groups. It is a land of tolerance, and religious fundamentalism can not continue for long in it. There are reactionary changes within religions and new sects are created. Sikhism is one such product. Naipaul regards it as a compromise between the Hindu and the Islamic orthodoxy. It originated in a period when national interests were superior to religious. It became more and more powerful and its glory culminated during the tenth Guru:

> Guru Nanak's illumination was the quietist one that there was a middle way: that there was no Hindu and no Muslim, that there could be a blending of the faiths. Islam had its fixed articles

> of faith, however, its fixed, pervasive rules - no room there for Nanak - like speculation and compromise. (*Million* 422)

Naipaul opines that India became progressive with the touch of the European culture and civilization. The Hindu India was complacent and stagnant. When it came into contact with the Western awakening it became progressive and open. During the British period a number of reformers, teachers and missionaries worked for the upliftment of the society. What Naipaul underlines is that interaction among religions creates progressive ideologies:

> For 150 years or more Hindu India - responding to the New Learning that had come to it with the British - had known reforming movements. For 150 years there had been a remarkable series of leaders and teachers and wise men, exceeded by no country in Asia. (423)

Naipaul has criticized not only Hinduism but also Islam unsparingly. His severe criticism of several Islamic attitudes has created a lot of controversy. He visited India with several pre-conceived notions but when he visited the non-Arab Islamic countries, he went with an open mind. He found that Islam had various shades in these different countries. While it was rigid at one place, it coped with progress at another. He criticizes Islam where it becomes anti-human and retrograde. Yashoda Bhat remarks:

> This was the opening up of an unfamiliar area which became a source for his next travelogue, *Among the Believers* (1981). It was the journey of an unbelieving observer among believers. A meaningful and revealing title, simple, though it is; it emerged as a thought - provoking and controversial book. (*Introduction* 122)

The idea of visiting the Islamic countries came to him during the Iranian Revolution. He was in U.S.A. at that time. After the overthrow of the Shah, the news about Iran still centred round the execution. He visited Iran at a time when most of the people were leaving that country. He found Islam very tyrannical in Iran. In the following lines he describes how strict and rigid the Iranians are in observing Ramadan:

> It was Ramadan, the month when Muslims fasted from sunrise to sunset; and in Qom, the city of mullahs and ayatollahs, it wasn't going to be possible to eat or drink. In some parts of the country – with the general Islamic excitement – people had been whipped for breaking the fast. (*Among* 9)

In 1979, the Shah was overthrown and there followed the period of Islamic rigidity or Islamic tyranny. Every kind of entertainment was banned. The Ayatollah Khomeini declared music as un-Islamic. Mixing of men and women was prohibited. Naipaul is critical of such rigidity. This kind of tyranny is against all democratic ideals. In such atmosphere no election can be meaningful. Naipaul describes the undue and fundamentalist rigidity of those days in these words:

> The Ayatollah Khomeini was reported to have outlawed music. And Islamic rules about women were being enforced again. Mixed bathing had been banned; Revolutionary Guards watched the beaches at the Caspian Sea resorts and separated the sexes. (20)

The Islamic tyranny does not tolerate protests. A thing which is against Islam directly and indirectly is crushed rudely. In "The Night Train from Mashhad" Naipaul describes such an incident. A student who was protesting against the closing of *Ayandegan* – a Marxist newspaper, pasted a leaf of paper on the iron gate of the university building. An ordinary workman came over to him and not only crossed the leaf with the mark of X but also slapped the student violently. Naipaul concludes that with all the talk of revolution, violence was still there in the air:

> A workman near a food stall at the edge of the pavement walked slowly over, drew a red hammer and sickle on the leaflet, crossed the whole sheet with an X, slapped the student twice, in the middle of the pavement crowd; and then, without hurry, taped up the defaced leaflet more securely. (61)

Among the Believers opens a new territory in Naipaul's writing. It is the account of a journey which is dedicated to the study of the minutes of Islam. Naipaul explores the effect of religion on individuals of various kinds. He finds that due to the clash between inherited traditions and the new ways of life, split personalities are very common. The force of tradition in Iran is so strong that the new changes are not easily digested. Kunjo Singh observes in the article "Reporting from the Journeys: V.S. Naipaul's *An Area of Darkness, India: A Wounded Civilization* and *Among the Believers*":

> The split personalities and the contradictions that he notices with so much irony, in the Iranians in the U.S., are not a mark of hypocrisy but the natural result of conflict between inherited traditions, culture and religion and an acquired way of life. (103)

In Pakistan, Naipaul found a different scene. It was a Country which was newly formed and which still had to develop itself as an independent nation. Islam was becoming a greater force everyday. It was not merely a religion but also a great social and political force. The fundamentalists were growing powerful. They used religion to raise or pull down political leaders. In the following lines Naipaul describes how Islam was being used against Bhutto:

> Various people in Pakistan were calling for stricter Islamic laws, and at the university of Karachi there

> had been a gunfight with Sten guns between students of the left and right - words which have to be defined in every country, and here meant, on the right, people who were against Mr. Bhutto and were using Islam to discredit him, ... (*Among* 85)

Pakistan was gaining reputation as a newly emerged Islamic nation with new hopes and apprehensions. It was becoming a pioneering Islamic nation in the twentieth century. About the different shades of Islam Naipaul observes that while in Shia Iran Ramadan is a month of mourning, for the Sunni Muslims of Pakistan, It is a happy month. In Pakistan Islam served as a great social force which joined people together:

> Islam was each man's salvation; It was also the faith itself, the Prophet's story; it was also the community, stitched together by innumerable communal acts and occasions. Unity, faith and discipline: that was the theme of Islam, ... (101)

The partition came to the British ruled India as a trauma. Several people shifted from one side to the other. Friends became enemies. They remembered their past as a nightmare. There is the example of Ahmed who wishes away his heroic past. He thinks that his past was not heroic but full of sin. Naipaul underlines the adverse effects of partition on the psyche of the two newly created nations:

> For seven years, until the creation of Pakistan in 1947, Ahmed had served in the Royal Indian Navy, the navy of undivided, British - ruled India. He had taken part in the Bombay naval mutiny of 1946. But, thirty years later, his naval memories were not heroic or political; they were memories of sin. (119)

Islam in Pakistan provides not only religious and social laws, but also legal laws which are, in fact, the laws of punishment. These laws are very stringent and, in several cases, inhuman. They include whipping and execution, in many cases before the common public. No proper legal process is followed. The order of law is, in fact, the disorder of law in Pakistan. There is a chapter "The Disorder of the Law" in the book in which Naipaul remarks critically and disparagingly about these laws:

> These last were hardly laws; they were more about punishments. Drinking was to be punished by eighty stripes. The punishment for illicit sex, for an adult Muslim, was to 'be stoned to death at a public place'; for a non-Muslim, a hundred-stripe public whipping, with the possibility of death for rape. (154)

Everyone in Pakistan is not a fanatic. There are rationalists also. Several of the young men of the new generation are reasonable about religion. They consider Prophet Mohammed as only a great man. They think his divinity as a later addition. In the chapter "Basics" Naipaul speaks of a doctor's son who is a rationalist. The doctor is very proud of him:

> In what way was the son a rationalist ? The son – called over by his father to speak for himself – said that his attitude to the Prophet was historical. The great and good man existed; people added the divinity later. (163)

Islam is full of subdivisions like any other religion. There are the Shias the Sunnis and the Ahmadis. The Ahmadis do not believe in the finality of the Prophet. They think that Ahmad is their true religious leader. He was born in India at a time when Islam was in a bad shape. He redeemed the decayed faith and restored purity to it. Naipaul holds the opinion that there are reactionary forces in every religion and they assert themselves by forming groups within the umbrella of the broad faith:

> Ahmad's followers, the Ahmadis, claimed that Ahmad had appeared to purify the decayed faith.

> To other Muslims this reverence for the Promised Messiah derogated from the Prophet's 'finality' as a prophet and was the blackest sort of blasphemy. (201)

In every religion it is believed that there will be the second coming of the Messiah for the purification of the faith. The Hindus believe that God comes on earth whenever religion is in peril. The Christian believe in the second coming of Christ. The Ahmadis also believe that Ahmad will return to purge Islam of all its impurity. Thus, there is an underlying similarity among all religions:

> The true prophecy, according to the Ahmadis, was that someone *like* Christ was going to come back to earth as the Promised Messiah, to cleanse religion at a time of darkness and restore the purity of Islam. And that man was Ahmad. (204)

In Malaysia, Islam is undergoing a change under progressive ideas. Although there are the orthodox Muslims who do not accept these changes, there are those who support them. The orthodox Malaysian finds himself out of paradise in a city. The conservative Malaysian considers the progressive changes in Islam as a kind of disease. But the fact is that changes are irresistible. Naipaul is full of praise for such changes. He finds Malaysia a place better, in many ways, than Iran and Pakistan:

> There the new Islamic movement among the young is seen by its enemies as nihilism; they call it 'the Malaysian disease'. So the Islamic passion of Pakistan, with its own special roots, converts and converts again, feeding other distresses. And the promise of political calamity spreads as good news. (215)

Nasar's family is sufficient to illustrate this change. His grandfather gave up religious teaching as he regarded it as a profession without dignity. He preferred to be a paddy farmer. His son and Nasar's father went a step ahead and became an officer in the Forestry Department. He sent Nasar to England for education. People with old views still find it difficult to adjust with modernity and the freedom associated with it:

> The modernization of Malaysia, if it is not checked, will follow the same pattern. We accept technology, but it must not affect the basis of the social structure. Free mixing and alcoholism are the great dangers. That goes with free mixing. Trust is the basis of family happiness. (232)

Shafi is Muslim who accepts changes gradually. Although he has a sense of loss, he is not against changes. He thinks that everything is not for material profit. He associates himself with the Islamic activities not for profit but to meet the requirements of the Islamic movement. His open mindedness is clear from the fact that he marries a girl from another state. None else in his family had done this before. In doing so, he was breaking his family tradition:

> She comes from a poor family, from another state. Which is breaking a tradition of my family. Because none of my family, none of my close relatives, got married to somebody from outside the state. My parents did not object. But I feel I have broken a tradition. (245)

People of extreme religious purity find themselves in isolation. In the chapter "Araby" Naipaul describes such a community. People of this community have no faith in modernity. They continue with their orthodox ways. They do not mix with people at large. They do not welcome visitors. Naipaul could reach them with great difficulty. One is reminded of the religious community described by Matthew Arnold in his poem "Grande Chartreuse". Malaysia is changing and one has either to change or to live in seclusion:

> There was an Islamic commune in Kuala Lumpur. The young Malays there were said to have rejected modern ways and modern goods; they farmed a little piece of land and lived, as they thought, like Arabs - old Arabs, not new Arabs. They did not welcome visitors. (251)

The young men who go to the Christian schools get secular education there. In Malaysia 'secular' is an undesirable word meaning western and atheistic. When these people come out of schools they find themselves confused. They find it difficult to remain in the mainstream of the Malaysian religious life. Mohammed is such a man. When he becomes a teacher, he finds it almost mandatory to know the minutes of Islam. Thus, in Malaysia the knowledge of Islam is still a pre-requisite for everyone:

> Secular was the bad word with these men: it meant worldly, atheistic, western, non-Malay. 'So when I graduated from the secondary school I was secular. In that way my life was more confused. I didn't know much about Islam. So my Islamic consciousness was less. So I began to study more when I started working as a teacher.' (269)

The section devoted to Indonesia is equally interesting. In the very first chapter "Assaults" Naipaul traces the history of Indonesia and its struggle for independence. The Dutch were replaced by the Japanese who placed Sukarno as president. In 1965, he was removed and the army began to rule with a lot of cruelty and suppression. The individual freedom was brutally crushed. It created a restlessness. People withdrew to leap forward with greater force. Naipaul speaks of the new Islam in these words:

> The restlessness is expressed by the new Islam, the Islam that is more than ritual, that speaks of the injustices done to Allah's creatures and of the satanic ways of worldly governments: the Islam

> that makes people withdraw, the more violently to leap forward. (281)

Naipaul explores Islam both as a philosopher and a man of practical approach. He finds that Islam is a global phenomenon shaping the twentieth century world politics. With all its involvement with the world politics, Islam is still a faith rigid in its basics. At places it has fallen into the grip of fundamentalism and fanaticism and, at others, it has opened itself to new ideologies like the Western and the Marxist. In the four countries he visits he meets various situations and characters which help him in carrying out his empirical study. About the worth of *Among the Believers* as an empirical study of Islam and its relevance in the modern context, Yashoda Bhat observes:

> *Among the Believers* ... becomes an empirical study of Islam through the situations and characters he encounters in these countries. This empirical study with philosophic and epistemological enquiries into the nature of Islamic civilization, has a significance in the modern context. (*Introduction* 123)

In Indonesia, the past survives but in a different way. There has been a long history of conversion. The old myths and legends survive but they have lost their original significance. Indra is there in pictures but he is not the Aryan god. He is a character from the Javanese puppet drama. The legend of the five Pandavas is still there but the Pandavas are not the original Hindu characters. In the new context they stand for five Islamic principles:

> To Prasojo, as well as to the driver of our car, this Indra was only a figure from the Javanese puppet drama. Prasojo began telling me a local Muslim legend of five Pandava brothers, who represented the five principles of Islam. And I don't believe Prasojo had an idea of the true wonder of the legend: ... (*Among* 299)

Naipaul wished to explore the nature of Islam in the Indonesian villages. He felt a pleasant shock to find that the rural religion was a composite faith. Islam like Christianity came to Indonesia from outside. In the villages there came into shape a faith which consisted of the Hindu, the Buddhist, the Muslim and the Christian concepts. The villagers lived with the mosque as well as the church. Krishna occupied their psyche. Thus, in the rural Indonesia everyone was a man of faith, acknowledging the worth of other faiths:

> The religion of the village was a composite religion; the idea of the good life was a composite idea. People lived with everything at once: the mosque, the church, Krishna, the rice goddess, a remnant of Hindu caste, the Buddhist idea of nirvana, the Muslim idea of paradise. (326)

In the chapter "Mental Training in Bandung" Imaduddin makes his appearance. He continues to be a major figure in *Beyond Belief*. He is an electrical engineer with an Arabic bent of mind. He thinks that Islam in Indonesia has to be purified. While the village people are tolerant, Imaduddin is rigid in his approach to Islam. He thinks that the Islamic laws must be implemented and the discrepancies must be removed. There is a clear contrast between his approach to Islam and that of the villagers:

> 'According to my understanding of Islam, I cannot own a stretch of land if I cannot cultivate it. Only Allah has that right. So if this is run as an Islamic state, the state should arrange the land so that landlordism cannot exist.' (350)

Naipaul finds that every Muslim in Indonesia is not rigid or fanatic. There are Muslims with open mind and revolutionary zeal. Behzad is one such enthusiast. He thinks that radical changes are the need of the day. His ideas are the products of the communist influence as he is the communist son of the communist father. He does not believe in the supreme authority of the Prophet. He is in favour of great changes even at the cost of numerous lives. Thus, there are the complacent Muslims, the rigid Muslims and the radical enthusiasts. This variety lends the nation a specific place in the Muslim world:

> Good Muslims believed that the best time in the world was the time of the Prophet and the first four good caliphs; Behzad believed that the best time was in Russia between 1917 and 1953. Darkness had been dispelled; an unjust society had been overthrown; and the jails and camps of Russia were full of the wicked. (354)

Naipaul has been criticised for his so called biased criticism of several Islamic tendencies and critics thinks that he travelled with fixed ideas. Every Muslim is not a fundamentalist and, therefore, Naipaul's criticism sounds prejudiced at various places. Salman Rushdie criticizes Naipaul for ignoring several Islamic features. But the fact remains that *Among the Believers* is a rare critical document, specially for the western reader. Its historical and sociological worth is beyond question. Yashoda Bhat remarks:

> *Among the Believers* has a basic validity and authenticity in the vision. It opens up a new vista to the western reader. Its position in the history of modern travel books is as "a document of historical, and sociological value ... (*Introduction* 127)

In *Beyond Belief* Naipaul continues his study of Islam, although he claims to be a finder of stories. Through these stories he explores the changing dimensions of Islam. The crossover from the classical world to Islam is going on in several societies. Islam is affecting the social and political life of various nations in a new way. It has emerged as a new force in the world, specially in the Islamic countries. Different people react to the same forces in a different way. As a writer Naipaul examines their responses with as open mind and a clear heart. In the Prologue to the book he writes:

> But in some of the cultures described in this book the crossover to Islam – and sometimes Christianity – is still going on. It is the extra drama in the background, like a cultural big bang, the steady grinding down of the old world. (*Beyond* 3)

Imaduddin reappears in this book. He believes that there is no contradiction between Islam and science. Islam was removed from science in the Spanish, the British and the Dutch periods. God created the world to be prosperous and full of knowledge. The first revelation to the Prophet was 'Read'. Imaduddin taught Islamic principles to the converted people in an apparently modern and secular way. But everyone knew that he was a thorough Muslim:

> Imaduddin gave un-Islamic and modern – sounding names to his Islamic ventures ... And since Imaduddin here was preaching to the converted ... everyone knew that those virtues were Islamic ones; and some of the young people even had supporting quotations from the Koran. (15)

In Indonesia, Islam was acquiring more than religious dimension. It was becoming a great force in the field of the Indonesian politics. Mr. Wahid recalls the Dutch days when there was full religious freedom but religion was far away from politics. His grandfather saw Islam as a moral code in those days. Things have changed a lot since then. Mr. Wahid is struck to find that Islam is so changed now. It has come nearer to politics as well as to science:

> ... the Muslims in Indonesia in 1935 under the Dutch had the liberty to implement the teachings of their religion. This means in my thinking that my grandfather saw Islam as a moral force, not as a political force exercised by the state. (35)

Conversion is a major theme in the book. There is a chapter "A Convert" in which Naipaul describes the conversion of an Oklahoman into a Muslim named Mohammed Adam Khalid. Naipaul points out that in the past the Indonesian government was neutral but now it claimed to serve the faith. The faith is described by Naipaul as capacious. Imaduddin is a learned man with sophisticated way of working. He is a missionary who regards conversion as a return or a coming back. Everyone is born a pure Muslim. If he is misled into other faith of faiths, he comes back when he realizes his fault:

> The conversion in the Menteng mosque of a young man from Oklahoma was full of historical linkages and ironies. But to see them required another vision of the world. Imaduddin's missionary world-view was simpler. Everyone was born a Muslim, without sin, he had said at the conversion ceremony. (52)

Fundamentalism is inherent in Islam. The converted people have to face several restrictions. They have to look towards the Arabs for every small thing. All the holy places of Muslims are in Arab. After conversion one has to bid farewell to one's past. He has to become a rigid Muslim. Naipaul criticizes the fundamentalism of Islam and the way it affects the converted:

> These sacred Arab places have to be the sacred places of all the converted peoples. Converted peoples have to strip themselves of their past; of converted peoples nothing is required but the purest faith (if such a thing can be arrived at), Islam, submission. It is the most uncompromising kind of imperialism. (72)

With the widening of horizons, fast changes were coming in. There was a sense of loss among the purists. They thought that with these wonderful changes Islam was losing purity and privacy. The pattern of living was changing and the old local rituals, which had immense emotional significance, were not untouched by these changes. The loss of the 'old world of feeling' created a kind of melancholy in the 'pure' Muslims. Linus is one such Muslim. In fact, he represents a whole class of Muslims like him:

> So, as in the section of *Pariyem's Confession* I had read, the *wayang* allied to different uses of day and night, different patterns of living, and very old local rituals – could release emotions that were not easy for the outsider to enter. This old world of feeling was dear to Linus, and it was something he felt was now being lost. (91)

That the things have changed a great deal is clear from the fact that there is more and more preaching in Mosques and on television now. It indicates to the fact that Islam is more closely linked with social and political forces now. There are morning lectures on television. These lectures are given by Imaduddin who has become a great political force. In his case, Islam is a means of exploiting religious sentiments for political gains:

> In the beginning these religious lectures were only once a week, Sunday for the Christians, Friday for the Muslims. Now it's every day for the Muslims, early-morning lectures.' Those early-morning lectures on television were Imaduddin's. (114)

In the chapter "Ghosts" Naipaul introduces the reader to another character Budi whose name is derived from that of Lord Buddha. In spite of his success in the field of technology, he is a pure Muslim. He follows the laws of his faith strictly. He prays five times a day and shuns meat imported from outside. His example clearly indicates that Islam is not in conflict with technology in Indonesia. Budi is reminiscent of the Indonesian past and his example shows how this past has merged into present in that country:

> And now, with his growing success in the computer field, he wasn't letting go. In fact, he was now more religious than his partner. He was praying five times a day. He didn't eat beef in hotels or restaurants because the meat there came from Australia, usually, and the animals wouldn't have been slaughtered in the Muslim way. (120)

Naipaul visits Iran again to study that country more closely. His view that Islam in Iran is more rigid and tyrannical than in Indonesia is confirmed. In the chapter "Mr. Jaffrey's Round Trip" Naipaul deals with the union of religion and politics in Iran. Ayatollah Khomeini symbolizes this union in the best way. He is the political as well as the spiritual leader of the state. Mr. Jaffrey is a rigid Muslim who finds himself quite uneasy in India as well as in Pakistan. It is only in the Shia Iran and under the leadership of Ayatollah that he finds himself at home. He is not alone of his kind, there is a whole class of people like him:

> ... it was hard to imagine a country in a higher state of religious excitement. (Going by an item in the *Tehran Times*, there was even an Islamic way of washing carpets now.) Iran under the Ayatollah should have been very close to Mr. Jaffrey's dream of the *jame towhidi*, the society of believers, the oneness of government and faith. (155)

Naipaul's visit to the Islamic countries was inspired by the happenings in Iran. The revolution in Iran and the rising of the Marxist forces attracted him to go to that country. He analyses the various shades of Islam in the four Islamic countries. There are varying forces and varying responses to the same forces. Himself a Hindu, Naipaul could afford to be a detached observer of Islam. His comments on the Iranian phenomenon are particularly thought provoking. Yashoda Bhat remarks that Iran is at the centre of his Islamic journey:

> ... Naipaul also sympathizes, paradoxically enough with the modernizing revolution and the spread of Marxist ideology. Within a span of seven months, Naipaul travelled to several Islamic countries - Iran, Pakistan, Malaysia and Indonesia, although the idea had originated when he was to think about the happenings in Iran. (*Introduction* 123)

In the chapter "Salt Land" Naipaul describes the disillusionment faced by Ali during the course of the Iranian Revolution. He had read extensively about the French and the Russian Revolutions. He cherished romantic and heroic ideas about a revolution but when he saw the ground reality in Iran, he was disappointed beyond limit. He was sad about the killings which took place during, and in the wake of, the Iranian Revolution. In place of creating progressive atmosphere, the Revolution gave birth to a new kind of Islamic fundamentalism:

> It was as though we were in a theatre, watching a concert, and we were happy that we were part of the theatre. We were the actors now. For years we had been reading about Danton and Robespierre. But now we were the actors. We never thought that those killings could start afterwards. (*Beyond* 181)

Ali was imprisoned several times. His ideals were put aside and he was valued for his money. In the end the cases against him were dismissed. In the course of the revolution the real aims were lost and the mullahs became more and more powerful. Ali could not gain sympathy even from the Marxists. He found himself lonely and lost. This sense of loss appeared even on the face of his wife. The mullah-judge announced his judgement in these words:

> The mullah-judge said, 'I am not a man of Islamic revolution. But I have made this revolution to bring Islam. There is a distinction between the two. I want to make a house in heaven. I don't want to

> make a house in hell. A rich man is not necessarily guilty, unless I find some guilt in him. (188-9)

The stories of Paydar and Abbas are equally interesting. Paydar joined the Communist Party with great expectations but he found only frustration there. In the beginning the Tudeh Communist Party assumed an Islamic look but later it moved along the Soviet formula. In Iran, this formula could not succeed. Paydar was left disillusioned. His was a lost case like Ali. In the following lines Naipaul describes how the Communist Movement in Iran destroyed itself and how Paydar lost way:

> ... in the early days of the revolution it was the policy of the party to adopt an Islamic camouflage. That was easy enough: the themes of justice and punishment and the wickedness of rulers were common to both ideologies. But the Tudeh party destroyed itself. It gave a Soviet-style apparatus to the Islamic revolution, and then it was destroyed by that apparatus. (190)

Abbas is a war veteran. He suffered two attacks, in one of which he lost his eyes. In spite of this, he continues to be a thorough Muslim. He says that he wants to serve God as a warrior. He prays to God to give him his eyesight so that he may go to the front and use his experiences as a war veteran for the cause of Islam. In the following lines he appears as a hero longing for adventure:

> There was singing and chanting as on the battlefield, and Abbas made a vow: 'Allah, I accept whatever you wish, and I like whatever you like. But I cannot tell a lie to you. I need my eyes. If you give me back my eyes. I will use them to go back to the front.' (205)

After the revolution people longed for freedom. In a referendum they voted for the Islamic Republic. They thought that only this could ensure freedom. But to their utter frustration there arose a system of Islamic fundamentalism in which there was one supreme leader whose authority was final. He was not to be questioned at any cost. Thus, the dream of freedom slowly disappeared in the darkness of religious fanaticism. Naipaul describes the breaking of this dream in these words:

> The principles of the Islamic Republic had been worked out now by the scholars, and this rule by Qum was one of the principles. It was an aspect of the fundamental idea of the Islamic state, the idea of the Leader and obedience to the Leader, which was now never to be questioned, even indirectly. (217)

However, Naipaul does not fail to notice the inherent simplicity of the Iranian people. The common Iranians are simple people who can easily be persuaded and misled. They do what others do without thinking about profit or loss. The religious leaders victimize these people by their sentimental slogans. Naipaul is full of sympathy for these people. In the following words he describes how they were misled into the so-called Iranian Revolution:

> The Iranians were simple people; they could be persuaded by skilled propaganda to demonstrate for anything; people had joined the demonstrations against the Shah not out of conviction, but simply to do what everybody else was doing. (241)

Towards the end of the section on Iran, Naipaul compares Iran with India. He finds that while with the arrival of the Britishers India became regenerated and awakened, Iran tended to be more and more retrograde. He finds similarity between the regimes of Jahangir of India and Shah Abbas of Iran but by the beginning of the twentieth century things were entirely different. Things went from bad to worse after the Iranian Revolution. The young generation was interested in the Arab ways. They also revelled in having and showing guns. Their fanatic zeal is expressed in these lines:

> Young boys like to play with guns. So they would take them to the mosques and they used to show them the Israeli Uzi sub-machine-gun and other guns. These boys were fascinated, and at the same time they chanted slogans and prayers while someone related the story of the martyrs of Kerbala. (251)

There arose several Islamic groups which looked like political parties. These groups exploited the innocent Iranians. The young villagers who came to cities felt cheated. The Shah had also claimed obedience but his days were different. The openness of his regime was gone. Iran was heading towards the Arabic Islam. In the new set up religion was exploited for politics and power. Even violence was a part of it. Thus, Iran was divided into two parts - the simple villagers and the clever manipulators:

> The younger generation of the farmers who had migrated to the cities realized that they were being cheated. More and more, from 1970 on, Islamic organizations started Mushrooming in universities and in every city. And especially in the bazaar. The Islamic organizations were acting as a replacement for political parties. (258)

In Pakistan, Naipaul found that Islam was undergoing the process of transformation. It was tending towards fundamental excesses. Naipaul is severely against fundamentalism. He thinks that it misleads man so much that he is far removed from his own self. It leads him to a world of false notions which are against the basics of faith. Thus, it is a kind of disease which is taking Islam into its grip. Fundamentalism is a threat to the civilized world and it is a great danger to Islam itself. Yashoda Bhat quotes Naipaul's following words regarding the state of Islam in Pakistan:

> It pushed men to an unappeasable faith; it violated the basic; it could never wall out the rest of the

> world. And I thought it was possible, looking not many steps ahead, to see how in Pakistan, by the very excesses of fundamentalism, Islam might be preparing its own transformation. (*Introduction* 124)

The creation of Pakistan took place on religious ground. It was considered as a great victory of faith. There was a sense of religious euphoria in which there was no future plan for the newly created nation. This sense of victory paved the way for fanaticism. Pakistan was developing into a nation of a different kind of faith. It was a faith in which everything was fair. Even fundamentalism was accepted as a weapon for the spread of faith and attainment of political power. Naipaul says that there were more Muslims in India but those in Pakistan were gradually becoming of a different kind:

> In fact, more Muslims were to be left behind in India than were to be in the new Muslim state. It seemed rather that, over and above any political aim, the new state was intended to be a triumph of the faith, a stake in the heart of old Hindustan. (*Beyond* 266)

Naipaul reads the mentality of the converted people in Pakistan. He finds that these people have no sense of history. They do not care for the glories of past. They do not associate themselves with the Moguls or the Britishers. Lack of education makes matters worse. He is shocked to find that the glorious monuments of the past are in a miserable and decaying state. Thus, a convert has a different mindset. He runs after the glories of Arabia:

> This was due in part to a general lack of education, the idea of earlier centuries that what no longer had a purpose no longer required attention. But there was also the Muslim convert's attitude to the land where he lives. To the convert his land is of no religious or historical importance; its relics are of no account; only the sands of Arabia are sacred. (274)

Naipaul analyses the growth of fundamentalism in Pakistan. There are several reasons. Lack of education and progressive ideas is one of them. The native fanaticism is aggravated by the influx of fundamentalist forces from Afghanistan. These forces work through the *Madrassas* or the fundamentalist Islamic schools. They make Pakistan the centre of fanatic activities and a threat to the neighbouring countries:

> So the Pathans today are in a much stronger position than the Baluch in Baluchistan. The Pathans brought with them their fundamentalist trend. *Madrassas* (Koranic schools) and so on-totally alien to the Baluch culture. This happened after the war. Friends still keep coming here and talking about how bad it's become. (310)

If partition came as a victory for some, it came as a trauma for others. In Pakistan, there arose a number of fundamentalist groups who claimed to be the only true believers. They acted as patrons of people and wanted them to obey their fanatic commands rigidly. Thus, Iqbal's casual dream was turning into a nightmare. These groups wanted to eliminate the past of the converted people. They forced them to be 'transparent'. All this gave Pakistan the look of the land of the fundamentalists:

> The fundamentalists wanted people to be transparent, pure, to be empty vessels for the faith. It was an impossibility: human beings could never be blanks in that way. But the various fundamentalist groups offered themselves as the pattern of goodness and purity. They offered themselves as true believers. (311)

These groups believed in raising *jihad* or the Islamic war. They thought that the Koran gave them the licence to be violent. Thus, violence was accepted as part of the Islamic agenda. The secular atmosphere was completely shattered. In their zeal they forgot that violence had to be checked at some point. Almost all the Hindus and Sikhs were either killed or chased away while in India millions of Muslims still remained. In this way religion was used to attain social and political power by fair or foul means. Naipaul describes their version of *jihad* in these words:

> The Koran lays great store by *jihad*. It is one of the saying of Mohammed - not in the Koran, it's one of the traditions - If you see an un-Islamic practice you stop it by force. If you not possess the power to stop it, you condemn it verbally. ... I think this tradition gives the Muslim licence to act violently. (327)

There is a chapter entitled "Ali's Footprint" in the book. In it Naipaul describes the typical Islamic tendency of erasing the past. The converted people are forced in several ways to forget their old faith and its associations. Naipaul critisises Islam severely for this. He gives the example of the Gauls who had a greater freedom under the Roman rule. They could recover their past easily. Things are different in Islam. Here the important things are the Arab faith, the Arab language and other Arab features. Thus, Islam constricts not only religious freedom but also the concept of the past:

> The Gauls, after five hundred years of Roman rule, could recover their old gods and reverences; those beliefs hadn't died; they lay just below the Roman surface. But Islam seeks as an article of the faith to erase the past; the believers in the end honour Arabia alone; they have nothing to return to. (354)

To encourage conversion temptation is given in several ways. A convert is made the leader of the Muslim congregation. This is part of an attempt to make him forget his past. But past is something hard and immortal. It continues to remain with the converted. Hindus of the low castes are given this temptation but their past clings to them. In the following lines Naipaul tells how a *nai* can still be recognized although it is long since he underwent conversion. The lines are from the chapter "From the North":

> Though the *koum* had been given the dignity of leading the Muslim congregation in prayer - as if in this new incarnation he destroyed older caste ideas - his other functions were still, after five hundred years, recognizably part of the old Hindu order. (341)

The condition of the *mohajirs* was still worse. When they shifted to Pakistan from India they had the feeling that they were returning to their true home in Sindh. But what they found was entirely different. They were alien people who found themselves in an alien land. This disillusionment led to a kind of war which lasted for almost ten years and claimed about twenty thousand lives. Thus, the dream of the migrated Indians was badly shattered and they were branded derogatively as *mohajirs*:

> They found that it belonged to someone else; and the people to whom it belonged were not willing to let go. They, the *mohajirs* became the fifth nationality of Pakistan, after the Baluchis, the Pathans, the Punjabis, and the Sindhis. They were a nationality without territory. (364)

Thus, in his assessment of Pakistan and the state of Islam in that country Naipaul finds that things are not heading towards the right direction. Islam was taking a confused shape and the country was not moving on the path of progress. There were no plans for future. The creation of Pakistan was wrongly taken as the victory of the faith and an end in itself. Therein lay the cause of Pakistan's retrograde and miserable condition.

Naipaul found Malaysia entirely different. Unlike Pakistan, it was moving on the path of progress and openness. Naipaul found that things had changed tremendously since 1979. Malaysia was no more a land of no time. The complacency had been replaced by the progressive march towards wealth and prosperity. It was now a land of steel and concrete and glass. Naipaul traces the family history of Nasar and finds that, generations back, his ancestors were people of staunch faith. Things changed from generation to generation and by the time of Nasar, secular education had got considerable weight. Apparently religion seemed to have receded to the background but, in a close observation, Naipaul found that religion was still the force which gave people 'the first push':

> Nasar felt he had been educated by the Muslim youth movement; and he remained loyal to that education. Power and authority might have brought out his latent qualities and made him what he was; but it had also to be said that religion had given him the important first push. (392)

Although Islam is the identity and strength of the Malaysian people, their past can easily be traced with all its Hindu and Buddhist associations. To be a Muslim is to belong to a big and powerful group. It provides a sense of security which is of a rare kind. But the past still lives in Malaysia. Its presence is felt in various customs and rituals. The Malaysian marriage customs are derived from the Hindu past. Thus, Islam has not eradicated the past in Malaysia:

> The marriage customs of Malays are derived from old Hindu customs. At an early stage gifts have to be exchanged between the families. If the girl's family sends five gifts, the boy's family has to send seven; there always has to be a difference of two. Symbolic things are sent: sweets, money. (403)

However, there are certain things in Islam which create doubts even in the purest Muslims. Polygamy and violence are some such things. Naipaul explains this through the examples of Rashid and Syed Alwi. Rashid is a Bomoh's son and a true muslim having faith in the benevolence of God. He finds Islam very inspiring. But when it comes to polygamy, he has his own differences. He is critical of even the Prophet for marrying more than four women. However, this practice is no hindrance in his devotion to Islam. In the following lines Naipaul describes how even a pure and staunch Muslim may have his own doubts:

> He didn't like the idea of polygamy and what he could gather from his reading about the position of women in Islam. He asked the Pathan girl why the Prophet had married more than four wives, and the Pathan girl couldn't answer. Still, he kept on reading the Koran, and it began to appeal to his heart. He felt humbled by it. (413)

Syed Alwi is another Muslim having firm faith in Islam. He has fascination for the simple village life of Malaysia. He finds Islam full of vitality. It is a way to find the meaning of life. He observed his father and found that he was a true Muslim who wanted to know the meaning of life. He had faith in Allah who, in his view, was the symbol of this meaning. However he was shocked to find a streak of violence in his father's behaviour. He is surprised at the existence of these two things together. On the one hand he believes in the benevolence of God and, on the other, he has doubts about the acceptability of violence in Islam:

> The search for Allah or God was the constant in both worlds, and probably the only thing that could exist in both worlds for him. Although it does not explain why he was violent, or explain such diametrically opposed behaviour. (427)

Alwi's father was a staunch believer. He studied too hard to find out the meaning of life. His hard studies had a telling effect upon his mind. He became a little abnormal mentally. There is a word for this kind of man in Malaysia - *gila-isin*. However, his father did not want to be known as a fanatic. Therefore, he concealed the fact of his hard studies from the public. His case is the example of an open-minded Muslim who wishes to be a true believer but not a blind follower of the faith:

> Syed Alwi said, 'My father was considered *gila-isin* because he was pursuing God or something like that. Though the idea of pursuing God was something that only some relatives knew. It was not spread out, just in case people might misinterpret it, and think that this *gila-isin* was a kind of punishment.' (431)

Naipaul's objective and pointed observations make *Beyond Belief* a rare document. A combination of reporting and narration makes it a work of rare merit. His criticism of Islam is free from bias. He becomes a part of the country he visits. He goes to the roots to find out the truth. He is a travel-writer who travels to the imperialistic centres as well as the pockets of primitivity with equal open-mindedness. Yashoda Bhat remarks:

> Travel-writing has remained a unique blend of objective, plain reportage and narration, (which it originally was) and has also become 'para ethnographic.' The journeys from imperial centres to pockets of primitivity or the reverse journey of the Third World people to the major metropolises of the world have these features. (*Introduction* 108)

Naipaul's exploration of Hinduism, Islam and Christianity is incisive. He finds faults with every religion but he is never forgetful of the merits of all of them. He finds Christianity the most congenial for the growth of progressive ideas. While Hinduism has lost much of its vitality, Islam has assumed varying shades in various parts of the world. It has tended towards fundamentalism in several parts of the world which is very alarming. Naipaul finds fundamentalism a threat to modern civilization. Naipaul's travelogues are valid as in them he assumes the simultaneous roles of the protagonist and narrator. Mohit K. Ray observes:

> ... even though this may mean to some, 'Western' absorption, or as Naipaul himself has characterized it, 'universal civilization.' It has been the quest of a life-time, a journey, a travel into self, time, and space, in which Naipaul, the author, the protagonist, the narrative voice, and the principal character have blended together, have coalesced. (*Vulcanisation* 202-3)

5

The Political Realities

Naipaul is an exceptionally great observer of the political reality. In his travelogues he combines reportage with sport and adventure. At the same time he presents an appreciation of life based on his passing impressions. His travelogues create in the reader an intense curiosity about the past. He studies the societies with their varied political systems and structures. He finds that the governments play varied roles which affect the concerned society considerably. His visits to the Third World countries have yielded documents of rare political value. In his travelogues he shows sympathy for the weak and concern for men, manners and the general growth of a society. Mallikarjun Patil observes:

> His travelogues depict the life he has seen in different parts of the world. The vivid accounts he narrates in the books also display Naipaul's knowledge of men and manners, culture and civilized or uncivilized way of life he has beholden. (*Travel* 145)

Naipaul's greatness lies in his observation of the political reality from his own diasporic angle. He does not possess the imperialist bias. He examines various nations and the growth of political systems in them as a neutral observer. In India he finds politics influenced considerably by the foreign impact. He finds Pakistan as a politically underdeveloped country. In the Islamic countries he finds religion as a greater force than politics. His non-fiction constitutes a corpus which replaces the Western critique of the Third World politics. About the true worth of his travelogues Manjit Inder Singh observes:

> In literature, arts and cinema, the process of a redefinition of historically and politically inscribed experience is the most significant today. Not surprisingly the British and Western European accents of universalism, continuity and religious emancipation are replaced by new and divergent strains that mark the reversal to the native, local, folk and regional cultural representations. (*Naipaul* 130)

In *The Middle Passage* Naipaul illustrates why the West Indian society is the way it is. An explanation is always a first step towards understanding and sympathy. He explores the role of the government there and finds that slavery, allied with Christianity did the greatest damage to the Negro by destroying his values and setting before him the ideals of white civilization. The civilization in the country is a form of behaviour represented by third-rate white people who have had a chance to grow prosperous in the West Indies in a way they would not in England. Between the Indians and the blacks there exists a kind of hostility. The blacks have a deep contempt for all that is white. The Indians hate the blacks for not being Indian. Such a society obviously has no inner values. It merely imitates its way of life from Western consumer society. It is confused by the glitter of luxuries. It admires those who make money and those who are good cricketers. When it comes to politics everyone speaks of nation and nationalism but no one is willing to surrender the privileges or even the separateness of the group. In his exploration of the postcolonial societies Naipaul finds that most of the governments have failed in the task of replacing the old system by a new and better one.

In his Indian trilogy Naipaul explores the Indian scene after independence. He is shocked to find that India is still full of darkness and its independence has not made the desired change. In fact, the British rule in India was of several advantages which could not be maintained or improved upon after the Indian independence. In place of developing their own political ideology, the Indians mimic the Britishers absurdly. Yashoda Bhat remarks:

> ... what he had desired to see and expected to see was an India revitalized, rejuvenated, but simultaneously preserving the ancient culture. His visits to Trinidad and India – both countries now living with a postcolonial scenario, had certain things in common. Naipaul finds that Indians like the West Indies people mimic the British. (*Introduction* 114)

The Indian caste system originated as a division of work but during the foreign rule it took a bad shape. It became rigid. It became a sign of pride and arrogance. It divided the society and weakened it. Even after independence its rigidness continued. In Trinidad things were better and the caste division was not so glaring. It has been the failure of the governments after the independence which could not make any successful attempt to eradicate this evil. In the following lines Naipaul compares India and the Indian community living in Trinidad, and finds the latter better:

> In India it implied a brutal division of labour; and at its centre, as I had never realized, lay the degradation of the latrine-cleaner. In India caste was unpleasant; I never wished to know what a man's caste was. (*Darkness* 29)

Naipaul is shocked by the Indian poverty. There is an old tradition of glorifying poverty in India. Even after independence this evil could not be eliminated. Naipaul criticizes Gandhi for making poverty look holy. India's poverty is so deep rooted that it is known all over the world as a typical Indian feature. Naipaul is critical of Prem Chand for sentimentalizing poverty. It is a major failure of the post-independence Indian governments that they have not succeeded in making poverty less apparent:

> India is the poorest country in the world. Therefore, to see its poverty is to make an observation of no value; a thousand newcomers to the country before you have seen and said as you. And not only newcomers. (41)

His visits to India left him completely disillusioned. He found India a nation full of darkness. India was far away from the light of civilization. He viewed the Indian poverty, illiteracy, ugly social and political realities and the overall backwardness with contempt. The Indian civilization according to him is a 'wounded' civilization. India is caught between two worlds, one dead the other not yet born. His disillusionment is constantly present in his works. His disillusionment continued with him all through his career. The following words collected from the Internet are notable:

> Though a regular visitor to India since the 1960s, he has arguably analysed India from an arms-length distance, in some cases initially with considerable distaste and later with grudging affection, and of late perhaps even with ungrudging affection. (*Wikipedia*)

Naipaul has been living in different worlds and these worlds have been reflected in his works. His experiences in these worlds form the basis of his works. He had a shocking experience in India which left him disillusioned. The idea of India handed down to him by his ancestors collided with his own shocking experiences. This clash was both shocking and disillusioning. Naipaul was left confused and he had to begin writing from 'nowhere'. Namrata Rathore Mahanta remarks in this connection:

> When faced with the real India, he felt the India within him falling apart, and the man and the writer had to come to terms with it. The unity of his world was lost forever and the writing had to begin from an impossible place: a place of an un-healing wound ... (*Trilogy* 26)

In India, Naipaul found that the politicians had no vision. They followed the British way blindly. They took pride in being the rulers and did nothing substantial for the public in the changed conditions. It marred much of the charm of independence. In fact, the Indian independence remained a political phenomenon and it was not reflected in the life of the common people. This mimicry led to a kind of political stagnation. Naipaul was shocked to find that India was still very much like a British colony:

> Now the Indian Government does the same. The British dug trenches. So they dig trenches in Delhi, but only symbolically, here and there, and dangerously, in public parks, below trees. The trenches answer the insatiable Indian need for open-air latrines. (*Darkness* 81)

During his first visit to India, Naipaul stayed as a paying guest in Delhi. He found that this whole city was crowded and busy. He noticed that everywhere there was the impact of the colonizers. There was no sign of new thought or vision. It seemed as if progress meant only crowding of people and a hectic way of life. Naipaul felt that the old city had lost its original shape and was now only a city which looked like any British town. In this crowd, scope for free thinking and free action was completely lost:

> It was in Delhi, the city of symbols, first of the British Raj and now of the independent Indian republic: a jungle of black-and-white noticeboards

> mushrooming out of feverish administrative activity, the Indian Council for this and Academy for that, the Ministry for this and the Department for that ... (85)

The working of the Indian bureaucracy is marked by cold sloth. The red tapism of the Indian offices is horrible, shocking and inhuman. In this respect they have taken no lesson from the Britishers who worked with a rare promptness. The common man has to suffer a great deal at the hands of the callous bureaucrats. The shocking thing is that in this delay no document or file is lost or forgotten. The reason behind this delay is nothing but callousness. A common Indian finds himself in a worse condition after independence as he has to suffer much for petty things:

> The Indian bureaucracy has its silences and delays, but it never loses or forgets any document; and it was with pure geniality that I was hustled, as the writer of an unsolicited letter of praise, into the picture-hung office of Mr.Madan, the director. (124)

Naipaul found the Indian governments having no sense of responsibility. Everywhere there was chaos and mismanagement. These governments had failed miserably in the task of inculcating in the public a sense of duty and responsibility. On his pilgrimage to the holy cave of Amarnath he found that there was no proper arrangement for the pilgrims. The journey was horrible. There was dust and mud. Nobody was there to help the pilgrims. Nowhere in the West such a scene could have been seen:

> Dust overcame the dampness below wet rock; dust powdered the hard snow in gullies. Over one such gully a skull-capped Kashmiri had made himself the harassed master. He had a spade and feverishly dug up snow, which he offered, for a few coins, to pilgrims. (171)

In India Naipaul found a horrible sense of complacency and despair. He found that these at become the part of the Indian philosophy. This despair was seen in the actions of the government as well as those of the common Indians. It led to passivity which made India retrograde. There was no marked progress in any field. The British rulers had given India all the basic things but the native rulers could not improve upon them. In several cases they could not even maintain them. Naipaul had fantastic ideas about India but when he came face to face with the Indian realities, fantasy was replaced by disillusionment:

> It was only in India that I was able to see this as part of the Indian ability to retreat, the ability genuinely not to see what was obvious: with others a foundation of neurosis, but with Indians only part of a greater philosophy of despair, leading to passivity, detachment, acceptance. (200)

After independence there came a horrible sense of complacency in India. In the joy of the victory the future was forgotten. The politicians paid no attention to developing a new political system to replace the old one. There was no new ideology to direct the nation. Even the merits of the old system were forgotten. Naipaul found India in almost the same miserable condition in which his ancestors had left a century ago. Pankaj Mishra remarks that Naipaul came to India with the hope of finding his roots but what he found was misery and shocking complacency:

> But the India Naipaul travelled to, in the last days of Nehru, was a country made complacent and sanctimonious by the victories of the freedom movement; and while expecting to find a vibrant postcolonial country with many human possibilities, Naipaul came across wretchedness of the sort his ancestors had escaped from almost a century ago. (*Writer* XI)

Naipaul found the Indian civilization decaying. The political decay was only a part of it. The politicians had no values and they were interested only in furthering their own selfish ends. They kept aloof from the public forming their elite group. The lack of vision was reflected in the working of the government. Naipaul found that there was no hope of progress in India. Without an ideology and a definite plan a nation can make no progress. Satish K. Harit observes in his article "V.S. Naipaul and Indian Psyche":

> Naipaul does not see any hope of change or progress of India. Crisis of India is neither political nor economical alone. He considers them as only aspects of the larger crisis, which is that of a decaying civilization, where only further swift decay can accelerate the process of regeneration. (82)

Intellectuals and scholars have seen the success of democracy in India with doubt and scepticism. Even the commoners think that the Indian politics is not heading in the right direction. The irresponsible politicians can not lead a nation in the right way. The irresponsible nature of these politicians is reflected in their daily activities. The political rallies and processions are a great problem to the common man. When a great leader visits a city, the life in it is put off rails. In the following lines Naipaul describes the trouble caused to the railway by the president's visit:

> Do you know what a presidential tour means for the railway administrator ? Altering time-tables. Re-routing. Going over the track inch by inch. ... And then going yourself on a decoy run a quarter of an hour ahead of the president's train. So that you get blown up first. (*Darkness* 236)

The first shock to the independent India came in the form of the Chinese invasion. It revealed the hollowness of the Indian politics. It also put a question mark on the

Indian foreign policy. It also revealed that India was not fit for modern warfare. The phase of euphoria that began with Indian independence was overshadowed by the dark clouds of despair. Naipaul describes how India had to eat a humble pie in that fatal incident in the chapter "Emergency" in these words:

> India did not qualify for modern warfare ... She continued to produce mainly politicians and speeches. Her 'industrialists' were mainly traders, importers of simple machinery, manufacturers under license. Her administration was still negative. It collected taxes, preserved order; and now to the passion of an aroused nation it could only respond with words. (253)

The rulers changed but India remained the same. There was no real freedom in India and democracy was only a mockery. The Indians lived like slaves who had developed the habit of living in subjection. The new politicians failed miserably in giving the true taste of freedom to the common Indians. In several ways they were worse than the British rulers as they behaved like tyrants towards their own countrymen. After a brief phase of bliss the ugly face of the Indian politics began to show itself clearly. The wise Indians found no difference in the two kinds of rulers. The so-called independence obtained in 1947 was only an illusion:

> The uncle, Narayan says, was 'anti-political and did not want me to be misled. He condemned all rulers, governments and administrative machinery as Satanic and saw no logic in seeking a change of rulers. (*Wounded* 11)

In Naipaul's view the independent India was not moving in the right direction. It was hanging between the past and the present, and it caused a lot of confusion. Its past was beyond recovery and its present was badly confused. These conditions put a question mark on its future. In the postcolonial scene it had to move in the right direction and with the right pace. What Naipaul noticed was that there was no clarity of vision in the Indian politicians. The true meaning of independence could not be realized even long after its attainment:

> But in independent India rebirth and growth have other meaning and call for another kind of effort. The modern world, after all, cannot be caricatured or conjured away; a pastoral past cannot be re-established. (31)

The Indian politics is marked by corruption and indiscipline. The politicians are steeped in corruption and this evil is taking a more and more horrible shape everyday. With this the politicians are an unruly lot. They are unprincipled. They have no sense of responsibility. They are not answerable to the public. Joined together the two evils make the Indian political scene quite hopeless. Naipaul thinks that the British rulers were far better and the native rulers are not their true inheritors:

> The political issues were real, but they obscured the bigger crisis. The corruption of which the opposition spoke and indiscipline of which the rulers spoke were both aspects of a moral chaos, and this could be traced back to the beginning, to Independence. (35)

After independence, the relationship between the government and the public changed considerable. The politicians mislead the public with statistics and confusing facts and figures. Statistics is the worst kind of lie. The politicians talk in percent and not in exact numbers. These data are not comprehensible for the public. In fact, at the bottom of all this is the dishonesty of the politicians and the government officials. In the following lines Naipaul describes how the public is misled by the confusing facts offered by the politicians:

> The government had brought electricity to the village five years before, the Patel said, and he thought that forty percent of the village now had electricity. It was interesting that he too had adopted the official habit of speaking in percentages rather than in old-fashioned numbers. (74)

The Indian governments have failed in maintaining law and order in the country. This failure has given rise to numours anti social and anti national movements. Naxalism is one such movement. It claims to be a movement of the peasants but the fact is that it is a terrorist movement supported from outside. Naipaul says that it is a dead movement but the truth is that it has not only continued but also spread in many new parts of India. It has become a threat to the national unity and sowereignity. Its revival and spread is a major failure of the Indian politics. In the following lines Naipaul calls it a dead movement but one can not agree with him:

> The movement is now dead. The reprisals, official and personal, continue. From time to time in the Indian press there is still an item about the killing or capture of 'Naxalites'. But social inquiry is outside the Indian tradition; journalism in India has always been considered a gracious form of clerkship; ... (80)

A major failure of the Indian rulers lies in their inability to check population growth. The enormously growing population has made poverty a permanent feature of the Indian life. Naipaul blames Gandhi for glorifying poverty. In fact, poverty is the worst evil in India. The cities are choked and the villages are like slums. The scene of poverty is so horrible that it makes all progress impossible. A great number of children are undernourished. Mothers suffer from malnutrition. Farmers look haggard. In these circumstances India can not grow:

> India is poor: the fact has only recently begun to

> be observed in India, with the great growth in population, the choking of the cities, the political assertiveness of industrial workers. To many Indians, however, poverty, just discovered, also seems to have just been created. (100-1)

Naipaul criticizes India for several reasons but his criticism is always without malice. He disagrees with several Indian views but he is never full of ill-will. He thinks it improper that Indians give food to animals in those plates which they use themselves. He does not approve of the Indian orthodoxy and complacency. His wish is to make India aware of its darkness so that it may get rid of it. Savitri Tripathi observes:

> ... V.S. Naipaul, the grandson of this family was not satisfied at all with Indian ways of living, speaks the truth without malice because perhaps he had 'Utopian view' in his mind. All this can be seen in his earlier novels on India. He writes: *It still horrifies me that people should put food for animals on plates they themselves use.* (Italics mine, *Soil* 218-19)

Naipaul opines that the Indian governments have not succeeded in giving the right kind of education to the people. Compared with the European standards the Indian education is not upto the mark. There is no well developed educational system in India. The old system needs revamping which is not done. This system produces only clerks and not men skilled in various occupations. It is education which prepares the foundation for the progress of a nation. In India education means learning certain fixed things by heart and not having any real practical skill:

> Instead, Indians say that they have become too educated for India. The opposite is usually true: they are not educated enough; they only want to repeat their lessons. The imported skills are rooted in nothing; they are skills separate from principles. (*Wounded* 114)

The ideals which were cherished during the freedom struggle were given up after independence. The politicians became arrogant and snobbish. Their white dress which was the symbol of service during the freedom movement became the symbol of power and snobbery after independence. They ran after power and paid no heed to people's welfare. With all this selfishness, they lacked the vision which is required for the proper growth of a nation. All these demerits made these politicians a burden on the public:

> An immovable government, one-party rule, a democratic system which engaged only a fraction of the population, a decadent Gandhianism expressed in the white homespun of the Congress politician, no longer the sign of service but the uniform of power, the very sigh of which could enrage, and now the Emergency, a censored press, secret arrests: it was easy to enter into the hysteria of the opposition man. (127-28)

Even in the days of the freedom struggle, Mahatma Gandhi was aware of the fact that India was not ready for self-government. There were several weaknesses and evils which had to be removed first. The social injustice, the untouchability, the divisive politics and the narrow-mindedness were some such evils. Naipaul thinks that the Indians could have easily taken a lesson from the Britishers but they failed in doing so. The British rulers set several good examples of excellent governance but they were not followed. It was only after independence that this failure was realized:

> ... at least some of the ambiguities of his early days in India can be traced back to his wish to repeat his South African racial-religious experience, to get away from the divisive politics of religion and caste and region: his seemingly perverse insistence that India was not ready for self-government, that India

> had to purge itself of its own injustices first ... (142)

India: A Million Mutinies Now is the third book of Naipaul's Indian trilogy. In this he continues to examine the Indian scene. It is generally believed that Naipaul's approach in this book is more comprehensive and many sided. During his exploration of India Naipaul makes several notable observations about the Indian politics and governments. Although his focus is on the various movements which have emerged in India, his remarks on the Indian politics are not difficult to find. Yashoda Bhat observes:

> ... *India: A Million Mutinies Now* also is a conglomeration of several approaches to enquiry. A voluminous and a very ambitious work, running into 520 pages, it is distinguished from his earlier two travel books about India by the wide coverage as well as by a change in his attitude towards the country. (*Introduction* 130)

When Naipaul visited India he noticed several changes which had taken place since his last visit. There was prosperity coming in. but with this prosperity several evils were also becoming apparent. In several cases the meaning of freedom was misinterpreted. There was no difference between politicians and thieves. The police was the worst. Instead of protecting the public and guarding the rule of law, it spread lawlessness and anarchy. The government was unable to check the lawlessness created by thieves, politicians and the police:

> Policeman, thief, and politician: the roles had become interchangeable. And with money - the money of which the crowded, ugly skyscraper towers of Bombay spoke-many long-buried particularities had been released. These disruptive, lesser loyalties-of region, caste, and clan-now played on the surface of Indian life. (*Million* 4)

With all these evils India was making progress. The old poverty was nowhere to be seen. In his earlier visits Naipaul had found a great majority of people famished and haggard. There was hardly enough food for them. India depended on foreign aid for food grains. In this visit Naipaul found that India had worked wonders with the green revolution. Almost everyone was well fed and well clad. The labour of four decades was showing its impact on the life of the common Indians:

> There were none of the walking skeletons, with their deranged eyes. The agricultural revolution was a reality here; the increased supply of food showed. Hundreds of thousands of people all over India, perhaps millions of people, had worked for this for four decades ... (149)

India was making amazing advancement in the field of science and technology. Industrialization was gaining momentum. In every field including space research, industry and cyber technology India was taking great strides. The old cities were completely changed now. They lost their pastoral shape and acquired technological dimensions. The city of Bangalore is the best example of this. Earlier it was the city of the maharajas but now it is ruled by technocrats:

> Every kind of scientific institution was in Bangalore. The tree-lined roads of the garden city of the maharajas were now full of the noise and smell and fumes of three - wheelers and cars. It was no longer a city for walking in. (150)

An average Indian is hardly aware of the political developments of the country. He is not aware of the minutes of the working of the government. He lives in a state of ignorance in which he is badly misled and exploited. He does not know the names of the president and the prime minister. During the elections he is forced by the politicians to vote in their favour and his freedom is completely lost. These conditions make him reluctant towards politics. He becomes habitual of living under a shadow. He does not bother about who is at the top of affairs:

> The average aspiration of the Indian is to grow under a shadow - and this is all right as long as someone else throws the shadow. ... That's how we got governed in the first place. The attitude is: "As long as the local environment is the same, I don't care who is running things at the top." (162)

Even in this book Naipaul observes that India has suffered badly under the foreign rule and the Indian civilization is badly wounded. It is a country overrun time and again by foreign armies. As a result the Indians have no sense of pride in their past. The monuments are not properly maintained and they are not considered the symbols of national pride. A major failure of the Indian governments has been their inability to utilize the energy of the Indian people properly. Naipaul is shocked to find that even after independence India could not recover from the losses it had incurred in the past:

> It was like the India which had been overrun again and again by this army and that; it was the India of unfinished monuments, of energy going to waste, creating an impression of randomness. That was a jungle, too. (170)

In this book Naipaul finds India changing fast. The winds of change blow fast making India look troubled and confused. In the final analysis Naipaul finds that this is nothing but a sign of growth. India is entering a new phase of self-awareness and awakening. The process of liberation did not come to an end with the attainment of independence. In fact, it is a prolonged process in which several changes come in. The million mutinies indicate towards a new growth of India. Shanthi Sivaraman observes in the article "V.S. Naipaul's *India: A Million Mutinies Now* - A Celebration":

> What Naipaul describes in this book is the direction from which the winds of change blow. If it was people at the top who worked towards the freedom of India, the liberating forces have worked their way down into the grass-roots level and changed the shape of disturbance. Nevertheless it is a forerunner of real growth. (138)

However, this opportunity of growth was not being fully utilized by the Indians. Naipaul found that the Indian politics was so unprincipled that no growth could be possible. The politicians were running after power and they were ready to use any means, fair or foul, for that purpose. All this created a state of chaos in which there were no friends and no enemies. The various political alliances were based on narrow selfish ends. In this selfishness even the most important national issues were relegated to the background. Nobody was thinking about the nation:

> The politics of the state, as reported in the newspapers, was opaque to the visitor. In the politics of alignment and realignment there were no principles or programmes. There were only enemies or allies: penguin politics. What was true of this state, Karnataka, was true of other states as well. (*Million* 192)

Most of the state governments were behaving in an irresponsible manner. They were not aware of even their primary duties towards the citizens. There was hardly any difference between the working of the government and that of the mafias. All this created a very hopeless scene. In this hopeless state there was hardly any hope of a bright future for India. The people of India were getting disillusioned with the politicians and the taste of freedom was gradually changing into a bitter experience:

> The government is deteriorating fast. It will not be able to come up to the expectations of the people,

> and therefore I see a deep-rooted chasm in the country. Utter chaos. Our government has become a sort of mafia – the politician, the government servant, and the trader, none of them primary producers. (444)

Naipaul reaches the conclusion that the greatness of India lies in its ability to absorb excesses. India gave everyone a chance to live freely, even with his excessive views. It was a nation which could contain within itself those extremes which could not exist in any other nation. The hope of a bright future lies in India's assimilating power. In the last chapter of the book titled "The House of the Lake" Naipaul concludes his observations on a note of optimism:

> The Indian Union gave people a second chance, calling them back from the excesses with which, in another century, or in other circumstances, they might have had to live: the destructive chauvinism of the Shiv Sena, the tyranny of many kinds of religious fundamentalism, the filmstar corruption and racial politics of the South, the pious Marxist idleness and nullity of Bengal. (518)

Naipaul's visits to the four non-Arab Islamic countries yielded two books *Among the Believers* and *Beyond Belief*. Both of them focus on his observations regarding Islam but, here and there, one catches glimpses of the political scenes in these countries. When he visited them for the first time, almost each of them was undergoing some or the other social and political upheaval. In this troubled condition Naipaul could observe those realities which might have remained unnoticed in times of peace. A study of *Among the Believers* is highly revealing so far as the working of the different governments is concerned. Yashoda Bhat observes:

> When he visited these countries, there was a turmoil of one sort or the other in each of these countries.

> There were American hostages in Teheran, Afghanistan was overrun by Soviet Union and there was martial rule in Pakistan. (*Introduction* 123)

In Iran, the government was working strictly according to the rules of Islam. Whatever it did was Islamic and whatever was done by others was non-Islamic. Islam was assuming a tyrannical dimension here. Naipaul observed the impact of Islam on the working of the Iranian government and found that it drew a great deal of its power from Islam. The union of religion and politics resulted in a new kind of political condition in Iran:

> But now, when the government is a Muslim and a national one, the enemy is busy plotting against us. And therefore staging strikes and sitins is religiously forbidden because they are against the principles of Islam. (*Among* 14)

During his travels Naipaul found that most of the governments were inadequate to the task of governing a nation. This was not the case only in India. It was a universal phenomenon which shocked every sensible man. In Iran the politicians were busy with their selfishness and religious rigidity. They paid no attention to the upliftment of the people. The villages were the sufferers. There were no roads and electricity was still far away. People had to face difficulties at every step. Agriculture was in a bad shape. Naipaul was shocked to see their backwardness in the background of the so-called twentieth century advancements:

> He was with his girl; with her he had a developed eye for injustice, a feeling for injustice being one of the things that bound them together. He told me - and translated what he had said for the girl - that seventy-five percent of the villages in Iran were without roads and electricity. (74)

Naipaul found the political condition of Iran comparable with that of Pakistan. In both the cases Islam was interfering with politics. In a way, it was governing politics. The so-called secularism was only a false notion. There was anarchy and confusion in both the countries. Islam was being used as a way to power. It imposed restrictions not only on the public but also on the governments. The freedom of the individual was lost in this mingling of politics and faith. The real issues were ignored and religious sentiments were provoked and exploited:

> How the world works is the concern of science, and how society is to be governed is the affair of politicians, but what the whole thing means is the main concern of Iran and Pakistan. Politics is combined with religion in Islam. Iran and Pakistan can join hands to prove to the world that Islam is not just a faith of the past, practising ancient rituals. (82)

In Pakistan faith smothered democracy. It began with religious restrictions and went upto the extinction of all democratic institutions. There was no democratic government and no laws. Islam was considered as a governing force complete in itself. In an atmosphere of religious fundamentalism no democratic rights could be preserved. The formation of Pakistan was regarded as a great triumph of Islam and no democratic development was thought necessary:

> But soon in Pakistan these negatives were to be added to: no political parties, no parliament, no dissent, no law courts. So existing institutions were deemed unIslamic and undermined or undone; the faith was asserted because only the faith seemed to be whole; and in the vacuum only the army could rule. (112)

The so-called democracy could easily be suspended as Islam was there as an alternative. The army could rule well. The mullahs could make laws to govern the nation in their own way. The patron of the Islamic fundamentalism in Pakistan was Maulana Maudoodi, a hypocrite who died in Boston. He did not agree upon a separate Muslim state within India. Pakistan was created and, very soon, it found itself in the grip of Islamic fanaticism. The political trend set by the Britishers was given up and there was nothing to replace it:

> But the state had to be governed, the people had to policed. Public floggings were decreed, and there was no nonsense this time about eye-witnesses. The army sent out whipping vans to the bazaars: instant law, Islam on wheels. Step by step, out of its Islamic striving, Pakistan had undone the rule of law it had inherited from the British, and replaced it with nothing. (159)

Malaysia was different from Iran and Pakistan. It was more open to the West. It was making material progress which was obvious specially in the urban Malaysia. It did not stick to the Arabic mode of Islam. People were enjoying themselves with the pleasures of money. They did not hesitate in following the West. The orthodox Islam existed only in the villages. Malaysia developed politically through a long process of struggle with the Chinese and the British. Even after freedom from these it continued to follow their ways, specially of the British. Naipaul says that the prosperous Malays were no different from the colonials:

> Money magnified the limitations of places like Malaysia, small, uneducated, and coming late to everything. Money - from oil, rubber, tin, palm oil - changed old ways. But money only turned people into buyers of imported goods, fixed the country in a dependent relationship with the developed world, kept all men colonials. (250)

In Indonesia, Naipaul found that the regime of Sukarno was replaced by that of the military which appeared as a great force on the political scene. While in Pakistan the military rule was suppressive, in Indonesia it marked a great progress. It ushered a new era of material progress and prosperity. There arose a generation of educated people who could think in a new way. Outwardly there was peace and stability but beneath these there was a great deal of unrest. It seemed as if the whole country longed for democracy and a greater political freedom. Naipaul noticed this unrest and felt that changes were inevitable:

> In this period of rest there has also grown up an educated generation, the first generation in fifty years to know stability. But the army rule chafes. And already - the trap of countries like Indonesia - with stability and growth there is restlessness. (280)

In Indonesia, as in any other Muslim country, Isam was badly overlapping politics. This created a kind of anarchy everywhere. Islam was not considered as a faith only. It was wrongly conceived as a political force which could provide solution to the burning issues of the present day world. This mingling created confusion in which politics was badly lost. In Naipaul's view religion and politics are two separate fields. Matters are made worse when there is the hypocritical talk of secularism all around. The Prophet can not be the ideal politician of today:

> This late twentieth-century Islam appeared to raise political issues. But it had the flaw of its origins - the flaw that ran right through Islamic history: to the political issues it raised it offered no political or practical solution. It offered only the faith. It offered only the Prophet, who would settle everything - but who had ceased to exist. This political Islam was rage, anarchy. (331)

Beyond Belief is the companion volume of *Among the Believers*. It begins with a section on Indonesia. Thus the book seems to be the continuation of the former volume ending with the section on Indonesia. Naipaul focuses on the condition of the converted people but glimpses of politics are not rare. The growing dependence of the government on Islam is evident. Through religion it easily gets the support of the masses which it badly needs. If the support of the faith is put aside, it becomes difficult for the politicians to command the masses. Thus, faith becomes an effective weapon in the hands of the politicians. The mental training schools of Imaduddin which were out of favour with the government gradually caught its attention due to their appeal to the masses:

> Once upon a time the government was nervous of the faith, and Imaduddin was a rebel. Now the government, though unchanged in its ruler and its political forms, said it served the faith, and Imaduddin had no trouble in making the faith serve the government. The faith was capacious; Imaduddin was learned; he didn't violate himself. (*Beyond* 48)

Naipaul found this tendency in Iran too. The secularism of Shah was no more the order of the day. It was replaced by the Islamic rigidity of Khomeini which demanded complete surrender. The followers of Khomeini thought that the secularism of Shah was not genuine as it contained within itself a lot of corruption and lawlessness. The followers of Khomeini were considered as the only pure Muslims. They thought that the rule of the faith could ensure social justice and the rule of the law. Islam provided the government with the power to confiscate illegal property. It put a strict check on various social and political evils. These people thought that good governance was impossible without the support of Islam. Naipaul is skeptical about this view:

> It could be said that the Shah also required people to submit; but the Shah ran a secular and corrupt tyranny; whereas now, in return for their surrender of everything, the people were made a gift of the almost unbearable beauty of 'pure Mohammadan

> Islam, Islam-e Nab', which the Imam Khomeini had wished for them. (163)

In Pakistan, the euphoria of freedom was soon replaced by religious fundamentalism. This fundamentalism intensified till it took the shape of political violence. Even this violence was considered as religious. Under General Zia Pakistan experienced its first taste of political terrorism. Political violence has increased considerably since that time and it is taking uglier shape everyday. Naipaul is surprised to find that even this violence is regarded as sacred. Under the name of religion the politicians settle their scores and fulfill their political ambitions. Such kind of politics can not be tolerated in the civilized world:

> The Raiwind gathering that year had come at a time when the country was having its first taste of religious terror, under General Zia. He had hanged Mr.Bhutto, the Friday sabbath man; he had gone then to Mecca to do the little pilgrimage, not the full one, but he had still come back with a hundred million dollars of Saudi money. (286)

Naipaul found Malaysia more open to the West than the other Muslim countries he visited. With the coming of the material prosperity there came numerous evils which Islam does not permit. These evils appeared in the working of the government also. There was a lot of corruption in the government dealings. Pure Islam existed somewhere else. The purist Muslims found it difficult to cope with these new evils. When they confronted reality, they felt badly shocked but they could not change the order of the day. Money and the benefits which come with it became more and more important, specially in the so-called open minded urban people. Politics was degenerating fast. The Islamic ideals were being pushed to the background although Islam was still indispensable for the Malaysians. The corruption in the government is evident in these words:

> I am involved in some government contracts, and business outside the government. There is a certain kind of behaviour which I will not condone. Corruption, giving commission under the counter, taking people out, giving them ladies, condoning immoral actions to get contracts. That is the test. The test for a Muslim is when they are confronted with reality and a choice to make. (392)

In *Finding the Centre* Naipaul presents a glimpse of the Ivory Coast. It is going through a phase of transformation and everything is being altered. The old capital Abidjan is being replaced by the new one Yamoussoukro. The old ethnic ways are given up in favour of modernity. The president has big ideas and plans for his nation. He wishes to make the new capital the great city of Africa. His dream has created brilliant modern buildings, a great golf course, a big hotel and his own grand palace. With all these he wishes to be a symbol of power. He keeps crocodiles to make a show of his power. Feeding these crocodiles is a sacred ritual which is performed with great pomp and show. The president is the representative of the new politicians who are more concerned about their powers than their duties:

> The feeding ritual takes place in the afternoon, in bright light. There are the cars, the tourists in bright clothes, the cameras. But the crocodiles are sacred. A live offering - a chicken - has to be made to them; it is part of the ritual. (*Finding* 91)

A study of Naipaul's travel writings reveals that he finds almost every government inadequate to its task. They suffer from deficiencies which are irreparable. In India, in the Muslim countries and in the Caribbean he finds almost similar political conditions. The politics of these countries is confused and directionless. The long colonial period left the political system of these countries crippled. Even after independence they failed to recover from the dependence syndrome. Naipaul's greatness is due to his dispassionate observations. His fault lies in his inability to notice the crippling effect of the colonial rule. Kunjo Singh observes:

> Dependence – political, economical, intellectual and psychological and self-contempt are invariably the mark of colonial societies, Naipaul is not unaware of this yet curiously fails to take this into consideration when he castigates third-world societies for their deficiencies. (*Reporting* 100-1)

6

Conclusion

A truly great writer transcends the limitations of place and time, and achieves universality. Naipaul has done this with exceptional success. He finds a rare joy in being a writer. His writings are always with a purpose. He has worked throughout his life to find meaning and worth of it. He is a writer who makes his best efforts to make his life and career both meaningful and worthy. He remains one of the most widely read and admired literary figures of the contemporary world. He has never been afraid to discuss the pains of his own position. V.S. Naipaul is a disillusioned romanticist who finds modern writers too egoistic, and modern critics too intellectual, to be able to relate literature to life. His non-fiction constitutes a dispassionate criticism of society. This criticism is often painful but it is always with great social relevance. Naipaul's ironic vision makes his criticism sharp. Naipaul's writings have attracted critics like Walsh, White, Paul Theroux, R.H. Lee and Karl Miller. His non-fiction makes good reading which is delightful to the scholars as well as to the common reader.

Travelogues constitute a major portion of Naipaul's non-fiction. This kind of writing gave new dimensions to his creativity. He found a new storehouse of experiences which he exploited for creative purpose. *The Middle Passage* was a kind of turning point which opened new vistas for him. Since then he continued to be an indefatigable traveller throughout his career as a writer. As a travel writer Naipaul is neither an escapist nor a romantic. He is a keen observer of the world around him. He notices facts, analysis them and presents them in his own literary way. He shows a rare wisdom in converting his travel experiences into rare documents of social criticism.

Naipaul is a detached observer of societies. He castigates these societies ruthlessly. Even in their postcolonial state they have failed in maintaining their dignity. He criticizes not only Trinidad and Tobago but also India, the country of his ancestors. He finds a palpable process of degradation going on in India. Evil works in various ways in this dark area. The nation suffers due to man's impure heart, evil nature and malpractices. Ramnath, Hiralal and Malhotra are the specimens of the typical Indians. Naipaul expresses his contempt for India unreservedly. He finds Indians greedy, ignorant and narrow-minded. One by one Naipaul portrays the areas of darkness that are prevalent in both urban and rural Hindustan.

Naipaul's criticism of the Muslim societies is equally objective and bold. He noticed the Iranians suffering from split personality and the Iranian society full of contradictions. While on the one hand Iran depended on the West, on the other, it was becoming a greater victim of the Islamic fundamentalism each day. He found an almost similar situation in Pakistan. Pakistan became a reality in 1947 but the initial euphoria subsided soon. The formation of Pakistan which must have been regarded a beginning, was mistaken for an end. No attempt was made in Pakistan to build up new institutions and a new civilization of its own. In Malaysia, people had lost their past and they had no definite vision of future. In big cities materialism replaced faith. Shafi is a representative of this lost generation. In Indonesia, Naipaul found that people were worried about reconstructing their past. This effort led them only to confusion.

Naipaul had the advantage of living in different continents and studying the society - individual relationship in different settings. He was in a state of voluntary exile throughout these journeys. He was at a distance everywhere. The privilege enabled him to study his own self as well as individuals like him. He pinpoints that writers, thinkers, prophets, fanatics and mutineers are the products of the varied social conditions. The influence of society is so overwhelming that none can escape it. Even trend-setters are the products of society. The social forces shape the individual according to the requirements of the society. Sometimes the same social conditions create varied personalities. The society - individual relationship differs from place to place and from person to person.

Naipaul's criticism of Hinduism, Islam and Christianity is incisive. He finds demerits in every religion but he is never forgetful of the merits of all of them. He finds Christianity the most suitable for the growth of progressive ideas. If Hinduism has lost much of its vitality, Islam has assumed varying shades in varying parts of the world. In several parts of the world it has tended towards fundamentalism, which is very alarming. The Islamic fundamentalism is a serious threat to the civilized world of today. So far as his own faith is concerned he is neither romantic nor sentimental about it. He is an equally ruthless critic of Hinduism. His understanding of India and Hinduism may not be perfect but his treatment of them is objective and unsparing. In fact, the Indian culture and civilization are so complex for him to present a perfectly accurate account of them. India is a land of tolerance and religious fundamentalism can not flourish in it. There are reactionary changes within religions and new faiths are created. Naipaul's travelogues are valid as in them he assumes the simultaneous roles of the protagonist and narrator.

As a traveller Naipaul never missed to observe the political realities which came accross him. Even in this field he is an adventurer. He offers an appreciation of life based on his passing impressions. His travelogues trace the political developments in the countries he visits incisively. He scrutinizes the societies with their varied political systems and structures. The governments play varied roles which affect the concerned society considerably. His travelogues are documents of rare political value. He examines various nations and the growth of political systems in them as a neutral observer. In India, he finds politics influenced considerably by the colonial rulers. He criticizes Pakistan as a politically under-developed country. In the Islamic countries religion is a greater force than politics. His observations successfully replace the Western critique of the Third World politics.

Naipaul's non-fiction is objective but it is never without the merits of fiction. He is great because he can successfully assume the varied roles of a prophet, a soothsayer, a doomwatcher, a journalist, a novelist and a ruthless critic. The awards he received conformed the acceptance of his vision and his art. He looked at the postcolonial societies with the Conradian vision. With this vision is combined the autobiographical element which distinguishes the Naipaul cannon. It is as a writer of rootlessness and the crisis of identity that he is best known in the literary world.

Naipaul is a nomadic writer and an expert interpreter of experiences. He is bold enough to write on controversial topics. He is more than a pamphleteer. He never shirks from unpleasant topics. He successfully solves many problems related to the cross-cultural confusion. In fact, he is a philosopher who works indefatigably for the betterment of mankind.

Naipaul is modern *philosophe* carrying on the tradition that started originally with *Lettres persanes* and *Candide*. In a vigilant style, which has been deservedly admired, he transforms rage into precision and allows events to speak with their own inherent irony. (*wikipedia*)

Bibliography

(a) Primary Sources:

Mishra, Pankaj. ed. *V.S. Naipaul: Literary Occasions - Essays.* London: Picador, 2004. Print.

——. ed. *V.S. Naipaul: The Writer and the World – Essays.* London: Picador, 2002. Print.

Naipaul, V.S. *Among the Believers – An Islamic Journey.* London: Andre Deutsch Ltd., 1981. Print.

——. *An Area of Darkness.* London: Picador, 1964. Print.

——. *Beyond Belief.* New Delhi: Penguin Books, 1998. Print.

——. *Finding the Centre – Two Narratives.* London: Andre Deutsch Ltd., 1984.Print.

——. *India: A Million Mutinies Now.* London: Vintage, 1998. Print.

——. *India: A Wounded Civilization.* London: Picador, 2001. Print.

——. The Loss of El Dorado – A Colonial History. London: Picador, 2001. Print.

——. *The Middle Passage.* London: Picador, 1962. Print.

——. *A Writer's People - Ways of Looking and Feeling.* London: Picador, 2007. Print.

(b) Secondary Sources:

Books

Bala, Suman. ed. *V.S. Naipaul: A Literary Response to the Nobel Laureate*. New Delhi: Khosla Publishing House, 2003. Print.

Bhat, Yashoda. *V.S. Naipaul: An Introduction*. New Delhi: B.R. Publishing Corporation, 2000. Print.

Mahanta, Namrata Rathore. *V.S. Naipaul: The Indian Trilogy*. New Delhi: Atlantic Publishers, 2004. Print.

Mittapalli, Rajeshwar & Hensen Michael. ed. *V.S. Naipaul – Fiction and Travel Writing*. New Delhi: Atlantic Publishers, 2002. Print.

Mohan, Champa Rao. *Postcolonial Situation in the Novels of V.S. Naipaul*. New Delhi: Atlantic Publishers, 2004. Print.

Panwar, Purabi. *India in the Works of Kipling , Forster, and Naipaul:Postcolonial Revaluations*. New Delhi: Pencraft International, 2000. Print.

Rao, C.R. Visweswara. ed. *Indian Writing Today*. New Delhi: IAES, 1996. Print.

Ray, Mohit K. ed. *V.S. Naipaul – Critical Essays* Vol. I - III. New Delhi: Atlantic Publishers, 2002. Print.

Singh, Manjit Inder. *V.S. Naipaul*. New Delhi: Rawat Publications, 2002. Print.

Articles & Reviews

Chakrabarti, Santosh. "Alienation and Home: A Study of A House for Mr. Biswas." *V.S. Naipaul – Critical Essays* Vol.III (2005): 45-52. Print.

Colon, Aida Luz Rodriguez. "V.S. Naipaul's Half a Life: Memory and the Myth of Origin." *V.S. Naipaul – Critical Essays* Vol. III 2005): 167-180. Print.

Dalleo, Rafe. "The World, The Text, and The Caribbean Writer: Representation in The Work of V.S.

Naipaul." *V.S. Naipaul – Critical Essays* Vol. I (2002): 1-16. Print.

Das, Bijay Kumar. "The Question of Identity:A Note on V.S. Naipaul's Travel – Writings on India and Trinidad." *V.S Naipaul – Critical Essays* Vol. I (2002): 149-162. Print.

Goldberg, M.A. "Chronology, Character and the Human Condition: A Reappraisal of the Modern Novel." *Critical Approaches to Fiction* (1968): 13-24. Print.

Harit, Satish K. "V.S. Naipaul and Indian Psyche." *V.S. Naipaul – Critical Essays* Vol. II (2002): 76-84. Print.

Iyer, N. Sharada. "A House for Mr. Biswas: A Study in Cultural Predicament." *V.S. Naipaul– Critical Essays* Vol.III (2005): 17-25. Print.

——. "Naipaul's India – An Area of Darkness." *V.S. Naipaul – Critical Essays* Vol. II (2002): 85-95. Print.

Kuortti, Joel. "Intercultural Identification and Salman Rushdie's The Satanic Verses." *Writers of the Indian Diaspora* (2001): 57-70. Print.

Lal, H. S. "Naipaul's Vision of Indian Diaspora and Trinity of Indian Travels." *V.S. Naipaul – A Literary Response to the Nobel Laureate* (2003): 46-51. Print.

Leusmann, Harald. "The Trails, Trials, and Tribulation of V.S. Naipaul." *V. S. Naipaul – Fiction and Travel Writing* (2002): 65-76. Print.

Mishra, Nanda Kishore. "Trajectory of Displacement: Expatriate Sensibility of V.S. Naipaul." *V.S. Naipaul – Critical Essays* Vol. III (2005): 147-155. Print.

Patil, Mallikarjun. "India and Nobel Laureate V.S. Naipaul." *V.S. Naipaul – Critical Essays* Vol. II (2002): 254-266. Print.

——. "Naipaul, V.S.: The Travel-Writer." *V.S. Naipaul – Critical Essays* Vol. II (2002): 143-156. Print.

Santiago, Serafin Roldan. "V.S. Naipaul's Vulcanisation of

Travel and Fiction Paradigms." *V.S. Naipaul – Critical Essays* Vol. I (2002): 170-205. Print.

Sharma, Lakshmi Kumari. "V.S. Naipaul: The Man and the Novelist." *V.S. Naipaul – A Literary Response to the Nobel Laureate* (2003): 26-30. Print.

Singh, Kunjo. "Reporting from the Journeys." *V.S. Naipaul –Critical Essays* (2002): 96-106. Print.

Sivaraman, Shanthi. "V.S. Naipaul's India: A Million Mutinies Now – A Celebration." *V.S. Naipaul – Critical Essays* Vol. II (2002): 135-142. Print.

Thieme, John. "Naipaul's Nobel." *V.S. Naipaul – Fiction and Travel Writing* (2002): 1-10. Print.

Tripathy, Savitri. "V.S. Naipaul's Such a Long Journey in Search of Soil and Roots: A Study of Half a Life." *V.S. Naipaul – A Literary Response to the Nobel Laureate* (2003): 218-224. Print.

Websites:

http://www.contemporarywriters.com Web.

http://www.kirjasto.sci Web.

http://nobelprize.org Web.

http://www.nytimes.com Web.

http://en.wikipedia.org Web.

Index